**W9-DET-749**

# The Bulimia Help Method

## A Revolutionary New
## Approach That Works

By Ali Kerr & Richard Kerr,
Co-authored by Catherine Liberty

Copyright © 2014 by Ali Kerr and Richard Kerr

All rights reserved. This book or any portion thereof may not be reproduced or used in any manner whatsoever without the express written permission of the publisher except for the use of brief quotations in a book review.

First Printing, 2014

Bulimia Help
10 Catter Gardens,
Milngavie,
Glasgow
G62 7RT
www.Bulimiahelp.org

Legal Disclaimer

This book is not intended as a substitute for the medical advice of physicians. The reader should regularly consult a physician in matters relating to his/her health and particularly with respect to any symptoms that may require diagnosis or medical attention.

The information provided in this book is designed to provide helpful information on the subjects discussed. This book is not meant to be used, nor should it be used, to diagnose or treat any medical condition. For diagnosis or treatment of any medical problem, consult your own physician. The publisher and author are not responsible for any specific health or allergy needs that may require medical supervision and are not liable for any damages or negative consequences from any treatment, action, application or preparation, to any person reading or following the information in this book. This book is sold with the understanding that the publisher is not engaged to render any type of psychological, medical, legal, or any other kind of professional advice.

Any recommendations described within should be tried only under the guidance of a licensed health-care practitioner. The author and publisher assume no responsibility for any outcome of the use of this book in self treatment or under the care of a licensed practitioner.

# When not to use self help

You should not use a self-help program if the following conditions apply:

- You have a serious physical illness that could be affected by a change in your eating habits
- You are pregnant and you have not consulted your obstetrician about using a self-help program
- You are severely depressed or demoralized
- You have other problems with impulse control, such as, problems with alcohol, drugs, or repeated self-harm
- You have anorexia
- You are severely underweight
- You are severely malnourished
- You are in physical pain.

If you have even the smallest suspicion that you are in medical danger, consult a physician immediately. Eating disorders can be deadly, and if you are already in trouble, you need medical attention, not self-help.

*To Nathan and Indiana*

# Contents

# Authors Note

Hi there,

My name is Ali Kerr. Welcome to the Bulimia Help Method. I'm excited that you found us because I know that if you want to recover from bulimia, we can help you.

Firstly I want to stress that this approach is vastly different from traditional treatment. We don't ask you to analyze your painful past experiences or ask you to examine any personality 'flaws' that may have led to your bulimia. In fact we do just one thing...

> **We show you how to eliminate binge urges and cravings for life by restoring your body's own natural food regulation system** *(that's just fancy wording for your hunger and satiety)*.

Of course, it's not as simple as that. If it was, we wouldn't have written a book about it.

Also, I want to be clear upfront. I'm not a doctor, nutritionist, dietician, psychologist, therapist or neuroscientist. I am simply a woman who had suffered from disordered eating and bulimia for 10 years (from 1995 to 2005). With my husband, we pioneered an alternative method to bulimia recovery.

My bulimia was quite severe. I was binging and purging at my worst up to 10 times a day. I lost my menstrual cycle, I became socially withdrawn and depressed. I also suffered from social anxiety, panic attacks, heart palpitations, bad teeth and severe food and body preoccupation. My life was an endless cycle of binging, purging then starving... binging, purging then starving... binging, purging then starving... Food was a war ground and hunger was my enemy. Normal life felt like a distant forgotten memory.

In 2003, I hit rock bottom. I couldn't do this any longer. I was determined to recover no matter what it took. I confessed to my partner about my bulimia and together we committed to recovery. Frustratingly, for a time, recovery remained elusive: therapy proved ineffective, the best my doctor could do was recommend antidepressants and inpatient treatment was too expensive.

So with nothing left to lose, we decided to take matters into our own hands. Utilizing our research skills developed at university, together we began researching, testing and questioning everything we could find about bulimia nervosa.

We went right back to the bare basics with the research in this field. We considered a range of views and approaches and experienced a few frustrating dead-ends, as well as some wonderful 'light bulb' moments (e.g. bulimia is not *all in the mind*). This journey eventually took years of research, but near the end we felt we had devised a recovery method that could really work and we later named this the 'Bulimia Help Method'.

By following this approach I noticed a radical reduction in the frequency and intensity of my binges. After 3 months I had completely stopped binging and purging and within 10 months I considered myself fully recovered.

Best of all, as I recovered, my energy and vitality grew. I was calmer, more balanced, more content and had a greater sense of well being. My inner strength and confidence dramatically improved. My passion and love for life flourished. It was remarkable. I have never looked back and I have been free from bulimia and all food issues ever since.

We decided to share the Bulimia Help Method with others and since 2007 over 12,000 sufferers of bulimia have passed through our recovery program. The feedback has been remarkable and the Bulimia Help Method is recommended by experts, doctors, eating disorder professionals and charities worldwide.

The reason I wrote the Bulimia Help Method is that this is the program that helped me recover and brought me back to health, and I want the same for you.

This book is the result of years of research and development by me and my husband Richard. Before I move on, I want to acknowledge his continued support, dedication and commitment in making the Bulimia Help Method a reality. This book is as much a result of his efforts as mine.

To your fantastic, amazing, adventurous, enlightening recovery!

Ali Kerr

# Get your recovery checklist...

I have prepared a complimentary, downloadable Recovery Checklist to support the steps contained in this book. Simply visit our web site and download the Recovery Checklist to help you keep track of where you are in recovery. Go to www.bulimiahelp.org/bonus right now and download your free copy so you have it in your hands before you turn another page. So, your first Action Step is to get your Checklist. Go ahead . . . I'll wait. . . .

# Some FAQs

## How do I follow the book

To get the most out of this book, you should read it from start to finish, take notes, and apply what you're learning as you go. Read over the book carefully, give yourself some time for the ideas to sink in, and remember to refer back to it regularly.

We have broken the recovery process into small steps. Please take one step at a time. If you are feeling overwhelmed or if you find a particular step too difficult, it's perfectly okay to go back a few steps and wait until you feel more confident before moving forward again.

## How long does recovery take?

Although everyone is different, in general it takes around 6 months for the binge urges to disappear and a further 6 months to rebuild your confidence around food. Many of our members feel as though they are fully recovered around the 12-18 month mark. If this sounds like a long time, please do not feel disheartened, what we are aiming for here is total recovery for life and you will start to notice the benefits of recovery almost immediately.

## Should I see a doctor?

It is strongly recommended that you see a doctor before undertaking any self-help treatments. This program is meant as general advice only. It's not a professional opinion. If you have a very low body weight or are underweight, have any deficiencies, intolerances or injuries that may affect your diet in any way, then you should make an appointment with your doctor. If you are vomiting frequently or taking large quantities of laxatives (especially if you are also underweight) you should have your fluid and electrolyte balance assessed.

Similarly, if you encounter complications with structured eating, such as oedema (swelling of extremities), chest pains, palpitations, aches, or severe gastric upset go to your doctor immediately. Complications are unlikely, but it's always best to check out any adverse reactions.

## If my bulimia doesn't fit the formal definition, will this still work?

It doesn't really matter if you only binge a few times a month or if your binges are relatively small. If you are experiencing bingeing and purging behaviors in any way then this program is for you.

## I have anorexia, will this program help?

Anorexia and bulimia are remarkably similar and many of the strategies outlined in this program would be beneficial for someone suffering from anorexia. However, the concern is that anorexia is a much more life threatening illness than bulimia. Therefore, someone suffering from anorexia needs urgent medical intervention, not self-help.

## What if I don't have to binge to want to purge?

For some, eating even the smallest amount of food can lead to purging. Don't worry, we also offer practical advice on how to address this issue throughout the program.

## How will I know when I am recovered?

You will know when you are recovered from bulimia when you no longer crave or desire to binge or purge on food.

## Do I need a therapist to use this program?

It is your personal preference. Throughout this book we will avoid in-depth personal assessments and analysis, (we find it's not really required for recovery). In saying that, this book can work as a great companion piece if you are currently working with a therapist.

## Can I use this program with a health professional?

Yes, this program can work as a companion piece with a health professional. Please inform your health professional that you intend to follow this program. Perhaps give them a copy of the book for them to consult.

## Where can I get more information?

You can get support and advice about all of the concepts I've laid out in this book at bulimiahelp.org.

# Understanding Bulimia

Living with bulimia is really tough. You feel compelled to binge on food that you must later purge. You feel ashamed, dirty, and try to hide your secret addiction. It digs into you, creating dark thoughts as it undercuts your self-esteem. Life simply becomes a tiring show, where you constantly put on a happy face to hide your dark secret.

You may have heard that it's impossible to recover from bulimia. You may have heard that you will have bulimia for the rest of your life. I'm telling you right now that this is just not true.

It doesn't matter how long you have had bulimia, or how intense your bulimia is, you can achieve a full recovery. There is such a thing as total recovery for life. I am not talking about "watch out, be careful, bulimia might come back to haunt you any day" type recovery. I am talking about a recovery that comes with 100% complete freedom from bulimia and food issues. Food can become just food. You can get your life back completely free from bulimia.

We have had just over 12,000 sufferers of bulimia pass through our recovery programs and the feedback has been remarkable

Here is just a small sample of the feedback we regularly receive on the Bulimia Help Method:

*"The Bulimia Help Method has saved my life. I don't say that lightly. I have been bulimic for 10 years and I have been full of despair. I thought I would never recover and this sad sham of a life was what mine would be. I have been to doctors, therapy, and read every self-help book; this was the first time anything worked. I finally have hope again!!!"* - Nadine

*"I am in a position to "graduate" from your recovery program. After over 45 years of disordered eating this is quite incredible! I would like to express my profound gratitude to you for compiling a system that works. Once more I have a potential to live life, be happy, healthy and help others along the way."* - Pat Mary

*"I've not purged in over 17 weeks! I've been bulimic for 26 years and have never gotten close to this amount of time away from it. Maybe a few weeks here and there, but I've never gone 17 weeks. I am also down 27lb and have got my blood pressure under control. I would never have believed it."* - Angela

(You can view more feedback here: **www.bulimiahelp.org/success-stories**).

All these people considered themselves lost cases when they came to us, yet now their symptoms have gone. They are not just managing their bulimia, they are fully recovered. Their lives have been transformed and the way they think and feel about themselves has dramatically improved.

I am telling you this because I want you to know that recovery is possible. I want you to be one of our success stories. I want you to start living the life you truly deserve.

This book will show you exactly what you need to do to recover. I will give you solid, tried and tested practical steps that work for recovery. No time wasting, no unnecessary content and no nonsense.

Of course this program is no quick fix. Recovery is a journey and change happens gradually with plenty of ups and downs along the way. Recovery requires a sustained effort and a lot of perseverance, but ultimately it will lead you to a life you never even dreamed would be possible.

I am certain the secret to your success lies within you. You will come to realize in your recovery, you have more power, more inner strength, and more motivation within you than you thought possible. It's okay if you don't feel this strength right now. This strength will grow as you continue on your journey toward recovery.

If you don't feel quite ready to start recovery, that is okay too. I think one of the most important things to understand right now is that you're never really going to feel 100% ready for recovery, no one does. So many times we convince ourselves that we should wait for the right moment, a time when we are less stressed or when life is less hectic to start recovery, but when you think like that you can end up putting off recovery forever. There will always be a reason to wait until next week or next month or next year.

Little by little, you're going to discover for yourself, just how amazing life can be when you're no longer a slave to bulimia. Recovery is so worth it, but I also want you to know that you are worth it. Give yourself a chance, make the commitment to start recovery now, today if possible. Your future self will definitely thank you for not putting this off any longer.

It's ok to be feeling a little skeptical right now. There is no harm in having a little bit of healthy skepticism to any recovery program. Although, I really want you come to the program with an open mind. Completely remove, or at least set aside any preconceived ideas that you have about bulimia and about your recovery. This program is different. Some of these concepts may be new to you, you may need to rethink a good deal of what you believe is true about eating and weight management. Please read through the book and if the information provided feels like the truth, then you can be fairly confident that this approach will work and is right for you. When something is true for you it will resonate with you at a deeper level. In your gut you will know it to be true.

This book will get you started on the road to a new you, free from bingeing and purging. All you have to do is make the decision to commit to your recovery. Go at your own pace, but stick with us and let the process be revealed to you step-by-step.

Everything we have learnt over the past 10 years helping sufferers overcome bulimia has been condensed into this book. To the best of our knowledge, the approach outlined in this book is the most effective way to overcome bulimia nervosa once and for all. I am honored to serve you and I hope these principles, strategies and steps make a true difference in your life.

I am very excited that you decided to join us in this life changing program.

So let's get started, shall we?

To begin with I want to give you a fresh perspective on your bulimia. A perspective that I believe is much more empowering, encouraging and hopeful than the traditional view of bulimia.

You may have heard the phrase 'bulimia is NOT about food'. Well, I disagree. I believe bulimia has a lot to do with food (after all, it is called an "eating" disorder). I believe that by neglecting the core issues of food and nutrition many bulimics fail to recover.

Lets look at some scientific evidence for further explanation....

## The Ancel Keys Semi Starvation Study

This is the only large scale, long-term scientific study to ever explore the effects of semi-starvation on humans. For obvious ethical reasons it wouldn't be allowed to happen today, but in the less "health and safety" conscious 1950s it was acceptable.

More than 100 men volunteered for the study as an alternative to military service; the 36 selected had the highest levels of physical and psychological health. They were put on calorie-restrictive diets of about 1,600 calorie/day for 6 months (which is more generous than many weight loss diets prescribe today). As the men lost weight, their physical endurance dropped by half and their reflexes became sluggish. The men's resting metabolic rates declined by 40%, their heart volume shrank by about 20%, their pulses slowed and their body temperatures dropped.

Physically they complained of:
- Feeling tired
- Feeling cold
- Feeling hungry
- Difficultly concentrating
- Impaired judgement and comprehension
- Dizzy spells
- Visual disturbances
- Ringing in their ears
- Tingling and numbing of their extremities
- Stomach aches
- Body aches and headaches
- Trouble sleeping
- Hair thinning
- Skin growing dry and thin...

The men had every physical indication of accelerated aging. But it was the psychological changes brought on by dieting that were the most profound and unexpected.

The men became:
- Nervous
- Anxious
- Apathetic
- Withdrawn
- Impatient
- Self-critical
- Moody
- Emotional
- Depressed

They had a distorted body image and they had feelings of being overweight.

One man experienced a number of periods in which his spirits were definitely high. These elated periods alternated with times in which he suffered, "a deep dark depression." Those who ate in the common dining room smuggled out bits of food and consumed them on their bunks in a long drawn-out ritual. One man chopped off three of his fingers with an axe and was unsure if he had done so intentionally or accidentally!

Food proved to be the main topic in conversation. Not only did they continually talk about food, but many of the participants started to read cookbooks, collect recipes (which were later pinned to the wall, replacing posters of women), and daydream about eating.

One man even began rummaging through garbage cans. This general tendency to hoard has been observed in starved anorexic patients (Crisp, Hsu, & Harding, 1980) and even in rats deprived of food (Fantino & Cabanac, 1980).

The consumption of coffee and tea increased so dramatically that the men had to be limited to 9 cups per day. Similarly, gum chewing became excessive and had to be limited after it was discovered that one man was chewing as many as 40 packages of gum a day and "developed a sore mouth from such continuous exercise."

Before meal serving time, the study participants would battle in their heads as to how they would eat their meal; either devour it or eat slowly savoring every mouthful. Many took an extraordinary amount of time to eat it, trying to make it last as long as possible.

It was reported that a number of the participants did binge. One man who worked in a grocery store owned up to eating several cookies, a sack of popcorn and even two overripe bananas. This man told of how he felt incredibly anxious following his binge and said that he was so disgusted with himself that he ended up vomiting.

1 in 5 of the participants found themselves experiencing unstable mental states that affected their daily functioning, despite being in perfect mental health prior to the study – and all that had changed was the way that they ate!

## The re-feeding phase

During the re-feeding phase of the experiment many of the men lost control of their appetites and "ate more or less continuously." Even after 12 weeks of re-feeding the men frequently complained of "increased hunger immediately following a large meal." Several men had spells of nausea and vomiting. One man was released from the experiment because he was unable to adhere to the diet. He repeatedly went through a cycle of eating tremendous quantities of food, becoming sick, and then starting all over again. Some of the men found it difficult to stop eating. Their daily intake commonly ranged between 8,000 and 10,000 calories, and their eating patterns were described as follows:

- "Subject No. 20 stuffs himself until he is bursting at the seams, to the point of being nearly sick and still feels hungry;
- No. 12 reported that he had to discipline himself to keep from eating so much as to become ill;
- No. 1 ate until he was uncomfortably full;
- Subject No. 30 had so little control over the mechanics of "piling it in" that he simply had to stay away from food because he could not find a point of satiation even when he was "full to the gills."
- "I ate practically all weekend," reported subject No. 26. Subject No. 26 would just as soon have eaten six meals instead of three."

(Keys, A., Brozek, J., Henschel, A., Mickelsen, O., & Taylor, H. L. (1950). The biology of human starvation).

After about 5 months of re-feeding, the majority of the men reported some normalization of their eating patterns; however, for others the extreme over-consumption persisted. With unlimited food and unrestricted eating, their weights plateaued and finally, about 9 months later, most had naturally returned to their initial weights without trying. This gave scientists one of the first demonstrations that each body has a natural, genetic set point. There was a fear with unrestrained eating 'that the men would continue to grow bigger' however, this never happened. As they regained their weight, the men's metabolisms increased and they returned to their initial weights without trying. The tests revealed that the men who appeared to be the most psychologically adjusted had a more severe reaction to the starvation diet.

## Impact of their study

This study proves that the effects of starvation are incredibly similar to that of eating disorders (Polivy & Herman, 1976). It also shows many of the symptoms that might have been thought to be specific to anorexia nervosa and bulimia nervosa are actually the results of starvation! (Pirke & Ploog, 1987).

Remember that these men (like the vast majority of people with eating disorders) didn't have traumatic upbringings, genetic disorders, or mental health issues prior to the study. Yet, once their food was restricted, they still managed to fall into the dark world of eating disorders. They suffered with anxiety, food obsession, binge eating, purging, and depression - all because their calories had been restricted to 1600 a day. Bear in mind many so-called "healthy" diets today advocate even lower calorie intakes than this.

# Food Restriction Leads to Bulimia

Here are a few more interesting facts about food restriction and eating disorders.

- Dieting is a primary trigger for the downward spiral into an eating disorder (Thompson & Sherman, 1993).
- Dieting and starvation are believed to be a trigger which switches on the biology and changes in the brain associated with the development of eating disorders. (All Party Parliamentary Group on Body Image "Reflections on Body Image", 2012).
- Severe dieters have already begun the process to an eating disorder (Patton, G. C., et al. 1999).
- Girls who severely dieted were 18 times more likely to develop an eating disorder within 6 months than those who did not diet (Patton, G. C., et al. 1999).
- It doesn't even have to be a severe diet - 2/3 of new cases of an eating disorder came from those who dieted moderately (Patton, G. C., et al. 1999).

This leads us to the simple conclusion that food restriction or dieting precedes the vast majority of eating disorders. Or more clearly: Food restriction is the number one cause of eating disorders. **Put simply, dieting causes bulimia!**

If you restrict your food intake you are susceptible to becoming bulimic. If the healthiest, happiest person on the planet restricted their food intake, they would make themselves susceptible to becoming bulimic.

If you had never restricted your food intake in the first place then the chances are that you would have never felt compelled to binge and purge, meaning you wouldn't now have bulimia. I know for some of you this may come as a bit of a surprise, but it's really that simple.

........................................................................................................

*"Being sold the message of dieting can produce drastic dieting which can lead to eating disorders. Getting rid of dieting could wipe out at least 70% of eating disorders", - Dr Adrienne Key, Royal College of Psychiatrists.*

........................................................................................................

Let's explore the relationship between restriction and eating disorders further. Let's break this down into simple stages to help you grasp how food restriction can lead to an eating disorder.

## Stage 1. You restrict your food intake.

There are many reasons why people choose to restrict their food intake.

These reasons include:
- Avoiding major food groups like carbohydrates or fats based on the misguided assumption that it is healthy to do so.
- Avoiding specific foods, or on rare occasions, entire food groups, due to food allergies and intolerances.
- Embarking on restrictive detox programs in the belief that it will be beneficial to overall health.
- A direct attempt to lose some weight (by far the most popular reason).

## Stage 2. You ignore your hunger pangs.

When your body is deprived of food, you start to feel hungry. Hunger is your body's way of telling you that its energy supplies are getting low and need to be replenished. For most of us hunger can be described as an empty, irritating, insecure feeling.

By eating food when we are hungry we not only provide our body with the fuel it needs for survival, we also elevate many "feel good" chemicals in our brains, like serotonin, dopamine and norepinephrine which help to replace those empty, insecure feelings with feelings of confidence, security and satisfaction. These feelings of emotional comfort and inner calm are one of the reasons why many of us are tempted to eat even when we are not hungry.

When you are actively restricting your food intake you may start to ignore your hunger pangs. As your body fights back with hunger, you fight back with denial, and so the war against yourself begins. For a short time you may even feel good for "controlling" your hunger in this way.

## Stage 3. You hit the weight loss plateau.

In the beginning, most diets do lead to some weight loss (although a considerable amount of this is a result of water loss rather than fat reduction). However, after a certain point, most people hit a weight loss plateau.

At a plateau, your weight stubbornly stays the same despite the fact that you're continuing to eat less food. Why? Well in response to restriction your body slows down its internal workings (basal metabolic rate, or BMR), and you expend less energy so that you can survive on fewer calories. Your basal metabolic rate accounts for about two-thirds of your body's total energy needs, so any change to your calorie intake at all can make a huge impact in your ability to lose weight.

At this stage, a lot of people grow tired of the deprivation and constant hunger involved in dieting, so they quit. However, people with perfectionist tendencies or those who have an urgent drive to lose weight often continue, which leads on to the next stage.

## Stage 4. Your hunger begins to fight back

As you continue to deprive your body of the food and basic nutrients that it needs for survival you begin to lose touch with the subtle sensations of hunger and satiety, and start to experience a new type of powerful, uncontrollable hunger.

You no longer feel mild hunger pangs, instead your hunger comes in sudden, erratic bursts. You feel panicked and scared by these intense episodes of hunger and you start to realize that it's becoming increasingly difficult to stay in control around food.

## Stage 5. You feel driven to binge on food.

Every cell in your body is now screaming out for you to EAT! You are unable to fight back any longer. You don't understand why food thoughts and cravings are taking over your life and you can no longer resist the urge to eat, no matter how hard you try.

Suddenly you find yourself bingeing on food. At this point it may feel like someone else has taken over your entire body. Part of you wants to eat and part of you desperately wants to stop eating.

Feeling this powerless around food and ultimately succumbing to those urges to binge eat can be a very frightening experience. At this stage people often say, "*All of a sudden the eating disorder took on a life of its own.*"

## Stage 6. Out of desperation, you purge.

After losing control and bingeing, intense feelings of fear, panic, disgust, failure and guilt drive you to find a new way to get rid of the food. You feel trapped and you are so desperately afraid of weight gain that you decide to purge. This could be in the form of self-induced vomiting, laxatives, diet pills, or excessive exercise.

Purging is such a horrible experience you may feel confident that there is no way you will ever do it again. But this is just like the smoker who finds their first cigarette disgusting and is confident that they won't become addicted. Like all smokers before them, eventually, to their total surprise, one day they wake up to discover they are hooked.

Alternatively you may feel like you have just discovered a clever new trick that will help you to maintain your weight, but it doesn't take long for the novelty to wear off.

## Stage 7. You get stuck in the bulimic cycle of bingeing and purging.

Many bulimics don't realize that purging encourages more bingeing.

The two main reasons for this are:
1.  Purging is a form of restriction. This makes you more malnourished and further drives your primal desire to binge on food.
2.  After a binge, your blood sugar levels increase rapidly and this causes your body to produce insulin. When you vomit, elevated levels of insulin in your body cause blood sugar levels to fall very rapidly to sub-normal levels. This extreme drop in blood sugar results in a message being sent to your brain that tells you more food is needed. This results in cravings for carbohydrate based foods rich in sugar and/or starch. If you have ever noticed stronger binge urges the day after vomiting, you now know that a drop in your blood sugar is driving you to eat more food.

Now your drive to binge on food is stronger than ever. It becomes harder and harder to resist. In time this leads to more frequent episodes of bingeing and purging.

## Stage 8. Bingeing and purging becomes an emotional crutch.

Bingeing on food can causes a flood of endorphins to surge through your brain, which can temporarily infuse you with a warm sense of numbness or euphoria. Over time, many claim that they binge on food just to experience the endorphin release that comes with it. This is similar to a smoker who craves a cigarette when they are feeling stressed.

Over time you begin to rely on the numbness that bingeing brings you as an emotional band aid. It blocks out uncomfortable thoughts and feelings and gives your mind a moments rest from suffering. After a while you begin to wonder how you could possibly manage uncomfortable emotions without a binge fix.

## Stage 9. You believe you are mentally ill.

Progressively declining health, constant anxiety, disgust, and slavery to food, not to mention mood swings, body dissatisfaction, food obsession and feeling like you're going mad, all take their toll. Your self-esteem plummets. Your confidence shatters and you worry for your health and your life.

You find it hard to face the reality of what your life has become and you mourn for your lost dreams and aspirations. Life becomes a desperate show of putting on your "happy face" for fear of anyone seeing the real you and discovering your dark secret.

You can easily be led to believe that there is something inherently wrong with you; that perhaps you have been born this way, that you are damaged, broken, or lack the strength and willpower to sustain a healthy, happy life, but nothing could be further from the truth!

You may even begin to believe that you have evil inside of you, especially if like many people, you feel as though your body and mind have been taken over by someone or something else. Many people invent their own dark little monster to blame, some bulimics call it "Mia", some call it the "bulimic monster."

But... there is no monster inside you, and you are not broken. What you are experiencing are the side effects which have occurred as an inevitable result of malnutrition and prolonged restriction.

## Stage 10. You try and fail to recover

You may attempt to stop bingeing by using willpower to resist the binge urge. You may believe that if you hold out long enough and ignore the urge to binge that it will disappear. The problem is that it doesn't go away. If you are not feeding your body the nutrients it needs and if you are continuing to restrict in any way, the binge urge will never disappear. In fact, it will only get stronger.

Willpower is helpful for recovery but only for short term goals and general motivation. No one has enough willpower to continually resist the urge to binge forever. It's just not possible. Eventually, no matter how determined you are, you will give in.

This is why the most fervent promises to stop bingeing, made in the heat of post-purge feelings, so often fail. No matter how hard we try, our natural defense mechanism (which ensures we eat enough) will override our desire to restrict our food intake. Each time your willpower fails (and it always does eventually) it further reinforces the belief that you are trapped and doomed to a life of bulimia.

## Stage 11. You eventually accept that you are bulimic.

There is a limit to how many times you can build up your hopes for recovery, only to suffer the pain of having them shattered again and again. Eventually, it feels easier to accept your life as a bulimic, rather than pushing yourself to suffer the additional heartache and misery of continually failing at recovery.

Over time you forget what it was like to have a normal relationship with food. You forget your old personality and the old you. You forget who you were without bulimia. It begins to feel like your life has always revolved around bingeing and purging and you accept this as your new reality.

# Your Body's Survival Mechanism to Eat

So why does your body create what seems like a huge "hunger monster" inside you that just wants to gorge on a ton of food?

Well, this is actually a basic and natural human survival mechanism. There is nothing wrong or weird about this type of hunger. In fact, it is healthy for your body's survival mechanism to kick in when it detects that something is wrong. This is happening because your body thinks that you are in the middle of a famine and it is doing everything it can to ensure you are eating enough food.

Let's explore a little further...

There are three essentials that we need in life to survive, these are:
1.  Air
2.  Water
3.  Food

If we do not get enough air, water or food then we will die. To prevent us from dying the human body naturally evolved powerful survival mechanisms over millions of years to ensure that we breathe, drink and eat.

Let's put it to the test. Try holding your breath for 45 seconds. Not only is it extremely uncomfortable, difficult and scary, but notice how your whole body and mind feel as if they have been taken over by a single thought...

# BREATHE!

The urge to breathe becomes stronger and stronger.
You become obsessed with air.
You want to binge on air.

Of course after a little time, you gave in and started to breathe again. If you didn't breathe you would have eventually passed out and naturally started breathing anyway. This is because your body's survival mechanisms override your brain and literally shut parts of it down. Your natural survival mechanisms are far more powerful than your thoughts and your willpower (the same reason why willpower alone doesn't work when you are trying to resist the urge to binge).

The same goes for water. We have all seen movies where someone is lost in the desert and all they can say is, "water, water" At that moment, if they were offered the choice between a million dollars or a jug of water, I'm pretty confident they would choose the water.

So why would it be any different if you deprived yourself of food? It's not. If anything it's more powerful. Let's look at some of the more powerful side effects of food restriction. Do any of them look familiar?

## Side Effects of Malnutrition

When you restrict your food intake your body will fight back. Here are a few of the things you can expect to experience when you are malnourished:

### Extremely powerful urges to binge on food

Just like holding your breath creates massive urges to breathe, restricting your food intake causes massive, scary, powerful urges to eat lots of food.

### Powerful cravings for energy dense foods

Your body wants calories so it craves energy dense foods. This is why foods like chocolate and cheesecake can be so appealing to you.

### An increased taste response to sugar

Normally too much sugar tastes sickeningly sweet, now it seems that you never reach the point where it isn't desirable. This is because your body has actually increased your taste response to sugar so you can eat more of it. It's just another one of your body's clever tricks to ensure you eat more calories.

A recent scientific study has shown clearly that when a group of normal weight individuals were given a sweet drink to consume, almost all of them lost the taste for it after a very short time. The underweight group however, continued to enjoy it for much longer. This explains why chronic dieters and bulimics can go on long binges of sweet foods.

........................................................................................................

*"So true. Amazing how I take it for granted, now that my sugar cravings are gone. I assumed everybody had the same response to sugar I did, and just had amazing willpower!" - Deborah*

........................................................................................................

### An insatiable appetite

You lose the ability to feel satisfied and this can be really scary. Where normally you would feel too full, now it seems like you are able to eat and eat and eat and never feel satisfied. Many different research studies have shown that after restrictive eating, most people find that they are unable to stop eating when full.

### Food obsession

Food is all you can think about, in your car going to and from work, while studying, watching TV, or chatting to friends. You may even have food related dreams.

### Cravings for stimulants

As your energy levels plummet, you turn to stimulants such as coffee, tea, and diet sodas to keep you going, or as a defence against "giving in" to food. They can't provide relief for long though because what you really need is food based energy.

### Changes to your brain chemistry

Whenever you restrict your food intake you suffer from a host of mental side effects too. Large-scale studies from reputable universities such as Harvard and Oxford have noted that people on diets can significantly deplete their serotonin levels within three weeks of dieting. Regardless of your life circumstances or accomplishments, when your serotonin levels drop, so do your feelings of self-esteem and overall happiness. As the brain continues to be starved it deteriorates further and becomes even more self-critical. This leads to outbreaks of unpleasant psychological problems such as obsessive and compulsive behaviour, depression, anxiety, cravings, general moodiness and poor motivation. Simply put... food restriction can, and does, make you miserable.

# So What Does This All Mean?

Ok, I know this can be a lot to take in. It can be hard to grasp that restriction can be held responsible for your eating disorder. But I really want you to open your mind. It is essential that you allow this new information to really sink in.

We truly believe that for the vast majority of people, bulimia is mainly a physical issue, rather than a mental one. Research shows that the effects of starvation are incredibly similar to that of eating disorders (Polivy & Herman, 1976). And that many of the symptoms that might have been thought to be specific to anorexia nervosa and bulimia nervosa are actually the results of starvation (Pirke & Ploog, 1987). This might help to explain why traditional treatments that focus only on the mental aspects of eating disorders aren't very effective. If bulimia is mostly a physical condition, you cannot possibly "think yourself" better. Try "thinking" a broken leg better. It won't get you very far.

One of the most effective trialled therapies for bulimia nervosa is cognitive behavioral therapy (CBT). Research has found that 40–60% of patients using cognitive behaviour therapy become symptom free (Barker, 2003). The problem with CBT is that the results are largely dependent upon how well the person is guided by their psychologist, and whether they are focusing on food, as well as thoughts. Most inpatient treatments do have a good success ratio, but they have a high relapse rate after 5 years.

Shockingly, studies show that no scientific evidence supports the idea that resolving underlying psychological problems leads to recovery (Walsh & Cameron, 2005). Despite this lack of evidence, many people remain absolutely convinced that bulimia can be healed by focusing on the mental aspects alone.

But the mind-body connection is profound, and it can not be ignored. For instance, right now an overwhelming amount of evidence shows that physical exercise works to alleviate low-mood, stress, anxiety, and depression (Otto & Smits, 2011). In fact, physical activity has been shown to consistently improve life satisfaction and psychological well-being (Carek, et al, 2011).

It's the same with bulimia. To recover you must focus on addressing the physical aspects. When you heal your body you will heal your mind. This is your primary concern and focus in recovery.

## "So are you saying I should not focus on addressing my emotional issues?"

I believe too many of us spend too much energy trying to resolve our underlying issues rather than focusing on what really works for recovery.

At any one time traditional therapy may ask you to:
- Analyze and improve your self-esteem.
- Analyze and improve your relationships.
- Love yourself more.
- Forgive yourself more.
- Stop judging yourself and others.
- Think positive thoughts.
- Unlock past hidden pains.
- Analyze your behaviors.

I have a few issues with this. Firstly it is very difficult to feel good about yourself when you suffer from an eating disorder. Being asked to have positive self-esteem and to love yourself unconditionally is challenging for anyone, but it is especially challenging if you're also suffering from the pain, anguish and misery that comes with an eating disorder.

Secondly, there is just no proof to support the fact that resolving your underlying psychological issues will lead you to recovery (Walsh & Cameron, 2005).

Thirdly, this approach to recovery further reinforces the idea that there is something inherently wrong with you (there isn't) and it teaches you to look at yourself as though you are faulty (you're not). If anything, this approach to recovery undermines your self-esteem and confidence further. If someone tells you every day that you are broken, weird, or faulty, it wouldn't take long before you start to believe it. This undermines you rather than empowering you.

Of course, I do agree that there is a need for you to express your emotions, rather than suppressing them and it's certainly true that a good therapist can play an important role in helping people to move forward with their lives. For example, many bulimics are chronic "people pleasers" and struggle to prioritize their own needs without feeling guilty, and therapy can certainly help with issues like this. However, I don't agree that this is the solution to recovering from an eating disorder. Once you are caught in the bulimia trap, certain practical steps need to be taken to end it. Standing up for yourself, and not trying to please everyone can form part of the healing process but it generally will not take you the full way to recovery.

## "Then why is bulimia labelled as a mental illness?"

People who believe that bulimia is a mental illness often feel trapped and powerless to change their lives. They feel that they are "destined" to suffer this way forever and that full recovery will never be possible for them but there is one very important thing that you need to understand.

**Bulimia leads to mental health issues, not the other way around!**

If bulimia was the result of a mental illness we would expect:
- "Mental health symptoms to arrive before the eating problem (they don't)
- The therapies that work on mental health problems should work on eating disorder patients (they don't)
- Limiting food intake not to be sufficient to induce the mental health symptoms (it is)
- Normalizing food intake enough would not be sufficient to eliminate the mental health symptoms (but it is)" (www.mando.se).

Being bulimic makes you anxious, depressed, miserable, compulsive and moody. Because of this, bulimia has been labelled as a mental illness.

The great news is that in recovery, all of the psychological side effects resulting from prolonged food restriction can be reversed. You should not feel hopeless or worry that just because bulimia is labelled as a mental illness that this somehow changes your ability to recover, because it doesn't.

## This theory puts all the pieces in place.

Believing that bulimia is a physical, biological condition does make a lot of sense.

Have you ever wondered why people with bulimia tend to be overachievers and perfectionists? Could it simply be that in general, they have more motivation and willpower to succeed at a diet? When most people give up dieting after a few days or weeks, they remain committed and determined and in turn they suffer the consequences.

34

Also, why do you think so many people with bulimia tend to be athletes and runners? Athletes experience intense pressure to keep their weight down as their performance depends on it. They are therefore more likely to push themselves harder at dieting and food restriction (when in reality they should be eating more to compensate for the extra energy expenditure) and in turn they suffer the consequences.

Finally, why do you think the majority of bulimics are either female, or male homosexuals? (http://www.anad.org) Society puts more pressure on these groups of people to be thin, therefore they put more pressure on themselves to restrict more when dieting and in turn they suffer the consequences.

**It's the same answer time and time again.**

I believe the reason these groups are at higher risk of developing an eating disorder has nothing to do their mental or emotional state and everything to do with the pressure they experience to restrict their food intake. Bulimia is a biological condition, not a mental one.

........................................................................................................

*"I am a member of a fitness forum and while checking out some posts I came upon a thread I hadn't seen before. Eating disorder support...hmm, have to check that out. Wow...what I found was a group of men...these are a group of bodybuilders, fitness experts, personal trainers, some of them military... All who had gone on some sort of extreme diet and suddenly were gripped by the symptoms of an eating disorder...*

*What hit me so profoundly was how confused some of them were..one said it felt like his body suddenly rebelled against him. Some of them had no idea how they had suddenly seemed to develop an eating disorder, and were in disbelief over it. Men who had no previous problem..hmm sounds familiar" - James*

........................................................................................................

## Did your bulimia start with a diet?

Think back to when your bulimia began. Were you restricting your food intake?

If the answer is yes, then perhaps it's time to accept the fact that food restriction is responsible for trapping you into the "binge/purge cycle" of bulimia. To escape from the "binge/purge cycle" and to recover from bulimia you need to undo the damage that restriction and malnutrition has caused.

## "Why doesn't everyone who restricts their food intake get bulimia?"

If you restricted your food intake in the past then you can point your finger to that as the reason why you have bulimia. It's true, not everyone who diets gets bulimia. Research shows that 35% of "normal dieters" progress to pathological dieting. Of those, 20-25% progress to partial or full syndrome eating disorders. (*Shisslak, C.M., Crago, M., & Estes, L.S. (1995). The spectrum of eating disturbances. International Journal of Eating Disorders, 18 (3), 209-219.*)

So then, why did you develop bulimia? Unfortunately science is still uncertain as to the exact reasons why some people are more prone than others to developing bulimia from food restriction (my non-scientific guess is because you simply pushed yourself harder at restriction). Although, in reality the reasons are not relevant for your recovery. For now you can just accept that you are more prone than others to developing bulimia. Not everyone who drinks becomes an alcoholic, some people are just more prone than others.

## "But I am not dieting any more, I am bingeing on food!"

Bingeing and purging on food is a form of food restriction in itself. This is important to keep in mind. I know you may feel like you are eating a lot of food with each binge but if it's followed by continual purging, either through fasting, excessive exercise, laxatives, or vomiting, there is a good chance that you're still malnourished.

By purging you are not giving your body the chance to properly digest your food, meaning, that you are not getting the nutrition your body craves. You are malnourished and this keeps the primal drive to binge on food alive. This can sound crazy, considering bulimics tend to eat a lot of food, but it's true.

## "So what does this all mean for my recovery?"

So what does this mean for your recovery? Why do I keep raving on about bulimia being a physical condition rather than a mental one?

Well, because this has the potential to offer a profound shift in your understanding and attitude towards bulimia, yourself and recovery. One that is much more empowering, encouraging, positive and actionable. Lets explore some of the outcomes of bulimia being mostly a physical condition.

### Your inability to stop bingeing is not based on some character flaw

The reason you cannot stop bingeing is because your body is malnourished which in turn has triggered a primal urge to binge on large quantities of food. You are just experiencing the very natural and normal side effects of a restrictive diet. If you are malnourished, you will binge, this will happen to anyone on the planet. This has nothing to do with who you are as a person. You are not weak, broken or faulty because you cannot stop bingeing on food.

### You have lots of willpower

The truth is bulimics tend to have lots of willpower. Probably more than most people. For most bulimics it was their strong willpower to succeed at food restriction that got them into trouble in the first place. The problem is that the primal urge to binge comes from the primitive brain which overrides your willpower (just like your urge to breathe overrides your willpower when holding your breath).

........................................................................................

*"This absolutely blew me away, I thought I had no willpower whatsoever but what I have learned in my recovery is that I have LOADS of willpower but it was useless because I was caught in the bulimia trap. Having willpower and being undernourished, even thoughts I was of normal weight, were two things that blew me away" - Claire S*

........................................................................................

### You can stop blaming yourself for your bulimia.

The diet failure rate is around 95%. This goes for all diet products and plans out there. Would you let a brain surgeon who had a 95% failure rate work on your brain? Would you get onto a plane that had a 95% chance of crashing? Of course not. Yet, when the diet fails or if we develop an eating disorder we blame ourselves. Or we blame our poor upbringing, our psychology or our genetics.

It's time to stop blaming yourself. Bulimia is not your fault. You simply didn't know food restriction could lead to an eating disorder. So try to stop blaming yourself. If you are looking for someone to blame, blame society and its unhealthy obsession with restrictive diets.

### You can stop inventing reasons for why you may have bulimia

Without knowing about the dangers of food restriction, some people desperately search their past or analyze themselves deeply in the hope of finding some clue as to why they have bulimia. This can easily lead them to "invent" a reason for why they may have an eating disorder. They believe their eating disorder protects them in some way or helps them deal with some past trauma.

The reality is that your bulimia doesn't need to have a function; it doesn't need to offer you any benefit, it doesn't have to fulfill some hidden need and you don't need to blame some past pain or trauma.

### Chances are there was never anything actually wrong with you in the first place

There doesn't have to be anything "wrong" with you to be susceptible to bulimia from food restriction. In the Ancel Keys Semi-Starvation Study it was the men who were physically and mentally strongest who suffered the greatest aversion to the starvation diet. Chances are there was absolutely nothing wrong with you before you restricted your food intake.

You don't need to sweat too much about why you decided to restrict in the first place

So why did you restrict your food intake in the first place? Was it because you had low self esteem, a dysfunctional upbringing or a poor body image? In truth the reasons why you decided to restrict in the first place usually doesn't matter too much for your recovery.

In general for most of you the reason why you decided to restrict your food intake in the first place is because you wanted to feel better about yourself. We are continually sold the false message that dieting will make us happier, so we go on a diet in the false hope that we will be happier (when in reality it makes us miserable and encourages eating disorders). Trying to make yourself happier is a normal thing to do. Who doesn't want to feel better about themselves at times? So don't beat yourself up for restricting your food intake in the first place whatever the reasons where. You are now armed with the knowledge of how dangerous dieting is and I hope in future you will seek more healthy ways to increase your wellbeing without dieting.

For some of you the reasons why you restricted in the first place may not even be relevant in your life anymore yet your bulimia continues to escalate.

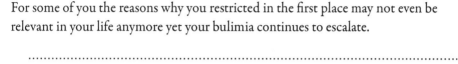

*"That is so true. In my experience, even my body image issues were not very strong after age 24 or so. But my bulimia lasted until age 33, long after the time that I accepted my body shape. True, I still had fear of weight gain, so there were some body image issues. But restricting food is what keeps the bulimic cycle in motion." -* Tara

Of course if there was a deeper more traumatic experience that you believe triggered you to restrict your food (sexual abuse, death of a spouse, etc.) then therapy and counseling may be essential in helping you to come to terms with those experiences.

**You don't need to resolve all of your underlying issues to recover**
The good news is that you don't have to build your confidence or improve your self-esteem in order to recover from bulimia. It actually happens the other way around. First recover from bulimia and then you will watch as your well-being soars.

Nourishing your body, stopping bingeing, and regaining your life from bulimia are the best things you can do if you want to rebuild your confidence and improve your self-esteem.

We have helped thousands of people overcome bulimia and many of them say that they can't believe the difference in their mental well-being once their bulimic behaviors stop. They feel so confident, positive and alive without ever engaging in therapy or analyzing their lives. Changes to your mental well-being will happen naturally, over the course of your recovery, without you even having to think about it!

So try to avoid thinking "I need to improve my self-esteem before I can recover." And don't convince yourself that you "have too many issues to ever recover from bulimia" because it's just not true. You don't need to resolve all of your emotional pain in order to recover.

## You are normal
Yes, you are normal.

........................................................................................................

*"There is nothing WRONG with you! You are not broken, weak, disgusting, or crazy. This is a problem - almost like a broken foot. It needs to heal, but it doesn't say anything about you as a human being. It feels like it does, but that is a LIE! It's not your fault (this was huge for me)." - Shanna*

........................................................................................................

## And the really big point is.... YOU CAN RECOVER!
Yes. You can recover. Your bulimia is mostly the result of malnutrition. If we address the malnutrition we go a long way to healing your eating disorder. This includes resolving any psychological issues you may have. Put simply, if we heal the body we can heal the mind. Isn't that good news?

We have had just over 12,000 sufferers of bulimia pass through our recovery programs and the feedback has been remarkable (You can view some of that feedback here: www.bulimiahelp.org/success-stories). All these people considered themselves lost cases when they came to us, yet now their symptoms have gone. They are not just managing their bulimia, they are fully recovered. Their lives have been transformed and the way they think and feel about themselves has dramatically improved.

I am telling you this because I want you to know that recovery is possible. I want you to be one of our success stories. I want you to start living the life you truly deserve.

## Take a moment...

Please take a moment to imagine for a second that there is nothing wrong with you, that you are absolutely perfect and that you are just experiencing the natural and very normal side effects of a restrictive diet.

- How would this make you feel?
- How would this change your view of yourself?
- Can you see how empowering this approach is?

The truth is, you are a perfectly beautiful person the way you are right now. You just happen to be suffering from an eating disorder.

I hope already you are feeling a little more optimistic and empowered about the possibility of real recovery. So now lets look at what we need to do to finally get this eating disorder out of your life once and for all...

# Recovery In A Nutshell

What's the difference between a person who has bulimia and a person who is not bulimic? The difference is that one binges and purges and the other doesn't. But wouldn't that mean that you are not bulimic 'in-between' bingeing and purging? Do you feel like a non-bulimic in between binging? For many the answer is certainly no.

So what's the real difference?

The difference is:
- A non-bulimic doesn't crave, desire or want to binge or purge
- A non-bulimic is completely free from the urge to binge or purge

Let's look at it this way: Imagine you're alone, bored and feeling down. You've had a stressful day and there is food in the cupboard but strangely you have absolutely no urge or desire to binge on food. Then would you binge? I am guessing not.

That would be like drinking 5 gallons of water even though you had no thirst or urge to do so. The point here is this: If you didn't experience an urge to binge. You wouldn't binge. Likewise if you didn't experience the urge to purge you wouldn't purge.

**It is the "urge" to binge and purge that makes you bulimic.** Our goal for recovery isn't just to stop you from bingeing and purging, we want to completely remove the urge or desire to ever binge and purge again. This is an important distinction and by removing the "urge" to binge and purge we help to ensure lifelong recovery.

Some recovery methods teach you strategies on how to manage the urges to binge and purge rather than remove them. For example, some encourage lifelong avoidance of potential trigger foods. The problem with this approach is that you may not feel like you are are fully recovered. You may feel like your eating disorder is a monkey you are carrying around on your back, ready to pounce on top of you in a moment of weakness. Even though you may not be bingeing and purging you will continue to have a deep seated fear of food. I would not call this recovery but maintenance. We do not want to maintain your eating disorder, we want to fully remove it from your life once and for all. To do this we need to remove the urge to binge and purge, not just to stop you bingeing and purging.

So let's learn a little more about the different types of "urges" people with bulimia experience.

## The Physical Binge Urge

Due to purging, restricting and not eating enough food your body is malnourished and this creates extremely powerful binge urges. This is the big one. All people with bulimia will experience this type of binge urge and it probably accounts for most of your binge urges. For some, curing this binge urge alone is enough for a full recovery.

To stop these massive hunger pangs, we simply need to teach our body that the famine is over. We do this by following a structured eating plan and it's the single most powerful thing you can do to recover fully.

## The Emotional Binge Urge

I know I have been hammering home that bulimia is mostly a physical issue, but there may be still a mental aspect. If you have had bulimia for a long time, you may be relying on it for emotional support. You may binge on food to quiet your mind or to eliminate uncomfortable feelings. We will be exploring strategies to overcome this binge urge in the stages, "Stopping Bingeing and Purging" and "Self Acceptance".

## The Urge to Purge

As well as removing the binge urges, we also want to remove the urge to purge. This urge is mostly created by the fear and anxiety of potential weight gain due to eating food. The good news is that purging is extremely ineffective for weight management and that we can stop purging and not gain any weight.

If eating food caused you the same amount of anxiety as breathing then you wouldn't really have a problem. You were not born with this fear of food, this is something you picked up over time. In the stages "Making Peace with food" and "Stopping Bingeing and Purging" we explore strategies to remove the fear induced by eating food.

## Overcoming bulimia for good.

Once we remove the urges to binge and purge you won't binge and purge. If you aren't bingeing and purging then you are no longer bulimic. And then you are recovered.

But that's not all... some of you may have been struggling with weight/ food issues for years prior to the onset of bulimia. Some of you may have never had a "normal" relationship with food. Perhaps you fear going back to your old eating habits, as you know they caused you the trouble in the first place.

This is where the 'Intuitive Eating' stage will really help you. In this stage you will learn how to stop relying on calories, food plans and food rules to dictate how you should eat and instead you will rely on your intuition. Intuitive eating is an extremely powerful and simple way to eat food that will allow you to maintain a healthy weight for life without any pain, suffering, rules or plans. I consider this stage to be the secret key to lifelong recovery from bulimia.

Don't worry if this all sounds a little unfamiliar at this point. Right now I just want to give you a simple brief outline. We will explore these concepts in more detail throughout the program. Just stick with us and it will become very clear.

But first before we start recovery we need to address some concerns you may have...

# Fear of Weight Gain

Being unwilling to eat properly due to fear of weight gain is the biggest reason people don't recover. So let's examine this more closely so that you get a good understanding of what happens to your weight in recovery.

I really want to stress that by following this program, although you may experience some temporary weight fluctuations, and although some of you may gain a little 'needed weight', your weight will not spiral out of control. Research shows that most people with bulimia (who are in the healthy weight range and who adopt regular eating habits and don't purge) end up within 1kg of where they started, and some even lose weight (http://www.cci.health.wa.gov.au).

This may come as a surprise to you that you can stop purging and not gain any weight. With any type of bingeing and purging, the chances are that you are consuming more calories than you would be if you didn't binge and just ate normal portions of food throughout the day. Purging doesn't help to control your weight and in fact, studies have shown that bingeing and purging can lead to weight gain (Agras and Apple, 1997). This isn't just for self induced vomiting either. All methods of purging are highly ineffective at removing calories from the body. Think of it this way: if purging was so effective why would most people with bulimia tend to be of average or above average weight?

Let's look individually at each of the more popular purging methods.

## Vomiting

In a study conducted at the Pittsburgh Human Feeding Laboratory, 18 bulimic women were asked to binge and vomit as they normally would, while the calories they consumed were carefully monitored. After vomiting, researchers calculated the amount of calories purged and compared it to the amount of calories eaten. They discovered that while the average binge consisted of 2131 calories, the women only managed to purge an average of 979 calories by vomiting. Even if you vomit immediately after a binge and try to empty all the stomach contents, (studies have proven) your body goes on to absorb at least 40% to 75% of the calories.

That means that following a binge/purge cycle, your body retains the calories equivalent to drinking 1.25 cups of honey (1200 calories). So, for all the pain, suffering, shame and disgust you go through, a large portion of calories will always remain. No matter how hard you try, your body will retain calories.

## Excessive Exercise

Muscle is the best natural fat burner you have and it helps to regulate your metabolism. Excessive exercise destroys muscle mass rather than building it, especially if your body isn't getting enough nutrition. This in turn actually lowers your metabolism, which encourages your body to retain more calories from any food consumed. In addition to this, excessive exercise increases hunger, which tends to result in more bingeing and purging.

## Laxatives

For weight loss, very few things are as ineffective as laxatives. Absorption of calories occurs high in the digestive system, whilst laxatives and diuretics influence the lower area.

After taking laxatives it may appear that you've lost weight, and you may even see the number on the weighing scales decrease, but any weight loss you do notice is due to water loss and dehydration only. It will rapidly return once you become rehydrated. Laxatives do not help you lose weight, they only help you visit the toilet.

## Diuretics

Diuretics have no effect whatsoever on calorie consumption. The only thing they do is make you lose water weight, which is quickly replenished when you drink again.

## Periods of fasting

Many people with bulimia engage in a period of fasting following an episode of binge eating. Fasting is considered to be another form of purging. Fasting is counter-productive for weight loss because it only ever serves to increase binge urges and uncontrolled eating in the long run.

## "Ok, so what weight will I be if I stop bingeing and purging?"

In general, people with bulimia tend to end up weighing roughly the same as they did before starting recovery however, it is important to take a couple of factors into consideration:

- If you are underweight at the start of recovery you need to be prepared to gain some "needed" weight.
- If you are overweight at the start of recovery you'll likely lose some weight during recovery, although weight loss tends to be very gradual.
- If you are within the "normal" weight range for your height and build then you may gain a little weight, but the chances are that you will end up at a very similar weight once you are fully recovered.

To get a really good understanding of where your weight will reside after recovery we need to explore Set Point Theory.

## So what is Set Point Theory?

Your height is your height. It's the way you were born and there isn't much you can do about it, so we just have to accept it. Well, the same principal applies to your weight.

Our weight has a natural genetic set point, this set point has a range that can swing between 5-10 lbs throughout our lives. Some of us have a heavy set point, some of us have a lighter set point, but most of us are somewhere in between. Set point is different for everyone and can be different for people of the same height. A very thin woman may appear underweight but this might be her natural set point – and the same goes for a larger woman.

Studies show that when a child is adopted into a family who already have biological children, they are not likely to take on the same physical characteristics as their adoptive parents in the same ways as those biological children do. If the parents are significantly overweight, it is likely that the biological children will also become overweight. But the adopted child does not seem to be affected by this environment.

Your body strongly defends your set point, so going below or above your natural weight range can kick start your body into a battle. Your body will resist the new weight and fight to get back to its comfort zone (Keesey 1993). Set point theory helps to explain why your body resists weight change and why is it so difficult for most people to become extremely thin.

Set points also tends to increase with age which is why it is unrealistic and probably unhealthy to aim to maintain your teenage weight in your 30s and 40s. A diet very high in fat and sugar and the presence of dieting in general, seem to promote a higher set point. Regular (healthy and appropriate) exercise can result in a lower set-point.

To really understand where your weight will be after recovery you need to try and understand what your personal set point is. If you have been struggling with bulimia, food restriction and weight issues for many years then it can be difficult to determine your set point. Observing your weight patterns over time gives an indication of what your natural weight may be. If your weight has gone up and down dramatically then your set point is probably somewhere in the middle.

To determine this further ask yourself: what kind of body type does your mother have? What about your father? Other family members? If your parents are heavy then the chances are that you will never be model thin as your genetic make up is a strong determinant of body size. When you are living at your set point, there should be no struggle to maintain your weight and you should feel at a normal weight that is right for you.

## To be truly free from bulimia you must accept and embrace your natural set point weight

Consider this: only about 5-10% of American women have the ultra-long and thin body-type that is seen almost exclusively in the media. It also helps to remember that the majority of the images you see in the media have been heavily edited, digitally touched up, stretched and airbrushed. It is an illusion, it is not reality.

Women and men who attempt to achieve this body type (but lack the genetic material to do so) are setting themselves up for a lifetime of yo-yo dieting, weight fluctuations, disordered eating and depression. The only way for life long happiness with food is to live at your ideal natural, healthy weight. By doing this you will feel stronger, fitter and better than you ever felt the entire time you were bulimic.

### "But, what if I don't want to live at my set point weight?"

It's okay to feel unsure about all of this right now. At first we all worry that we'll never be able to fully accept our normal, healthy set point weight. Imagining a life where you'll never diet again, where you no longer let the numbers on a scale judge your worth and where you've abandoned the pursuit of that "skinny ideal" can feel devastating too.

For a time it might even feel like you've given up on everything you ever believed in, but let me assure you that accepting your natural set point is not giving up. It is not failure or defeat. It is the biggest act of bravery and it will lead you to a lifetime of happiness.

The catch? You have to be willing to give it time. Give recovery six months of your life and see how you feel. Six months is a realistic time frame for change to happen, for initial weight fluctuations to even out, and for recovering bulimics to get past the difficult early months of recovery. Also, give it six months to decide whether this is a better way to live the rest of your life. Trust me, you'll be surprised by how quickly you adapt.

## Temporary Weight Fluctuations And Other Concerns

It is likely that you'll experience some weight fluctuations during recovery and it's important to be prepared for this. This tends to happen irrespective of whether or not you are below or above your set point weight. If your weight increases, do not panic - this is just a part of recovery. In time it will likely decrease again. It is very important that you do not let any temporary fluctuations throw you off recovery.

Due to restriction your metabolism may have slowed down a little and once you increase your calorie intake you may gain a little temporary weight. This can be a really challenging time, but after a period of increased intake your metabolism will fire up. This increases your energy expenditure and it will start burning the extra calories.

Also during the first few weeks of recovery you can expect to experience bloating as your body rehydrates and gets used to digesting food properly again. This bloating can cause the number on the scale to increase, but it is important to know that this is not a sign you're gaining any fat. After this, weight fluctuations can continue for around six months (sometimes a little longer if you're still experiencing relapses).

I know the idea of this is scary, but we have to be willing to give our bodies the time to rebalance. Eventually your metabolism will speed up again, you'll stop retaining so much water and your body will get used to digesting food properly again - which in turn will help you to find your healthy, natural set point weight.

*"When I started the program I was at the very lowest point on the BMI medium scale, a couple of kg lower than my usual bulimic weight. In less than 2 months from starting recovery I did gain, quite a few, almost 10 kg. Ok I'll be honest, I thought the whole part on the Set Point weight was nonsense, a clever trick to help us through recovery and that instead I would become as big as a house. Well it did not happen. My weight did increase (and it did very quickly) but then it just stopped . Today the weight I did gain has come off, by itself. It just settled out.*

*Today I weigh 2-3 kg more than my bulimic weight and I am eating anything I want when I want it. But, even if I weighed more I wouldn't care less because a life without bulimia is worth any number on the scale. The most astonishing thing of the whole story is that todays weight is my weight back in 1989 when I decided to put myself on a diet, lost over 10 kg and became bulimic. Bulimia is such an evil disease and it is totally ineffective in controlling weight. Hard to believe for a bulimic, but this is the truth." - Calandra*

## "Should I have a goal weight in recovery?"

It is very common for bulimics to plan to lose a certain amount of weight before starting recovery, or to have a target recovery weight, but this is a bad idea. Any goal weight will only encourage food restriction and will keep your bulimia alive.

"I thought I would lose weight till I was like 5 kg under my healthy weight, then try and recover, but it was impossible for me to lose those 5 kg, and it actually fueled my bulimia more. So I can tell you from experience, it won't work!" - Jan

## "Have I ruined my metabolism?"

There is no evidence to suggest that metabolism is permanently lowered due to disordered eating and many scientific studies have actually shown that our basic metabolic rate returns to normal following recovery from an eating disorder (Dellave, Policastro and Hoffman, 2009). One study even found that found basic metabolic rate can increase significantly (anywhere between 72% to 85%) within the first two weeks of recovery (Schebendach, et al, 1997).

The bottom line is this - If you feed your body enough fuel then your 'energy thermostat' will always reset itself in time. Though you must give it time to reset. We recommend at least six months. If you look at the big picture six months is such a small time compared to a lifetime free from bulimia.

.................................................................................

*"I remember starting recovery saying I'd only do it if I didn't gain weight, that I was only willing to recover if I could stay at the size I was. But you know what? No matter how ingrained those things are, you may surprise yourself as you continue to recover. Once I saw how amazing life was without bulimia I knew nothing would make me turn back, especially not the number on the scale." - Ali*

.................................................................................

# Support In Recovery

Many people with bulimia attempt to recover on their own first before seeking help. Some are able to successfully recover independently, but others need the support of a professional, a mentor, a loved one or all three.

While no one can walk the pathway to wellness for you, it is important to remind yourself that you do not have to walk this path alone. Support and understanding from those around you can be a powerful tool in recovery, especially as living with an eating disorder can be so isolating.

You've probably heard the saying, "a problem shared is a problem halved" right? Well there tends to be a lot of truth in that. Just talking to someone about what you're going through can help lighten the burden of bulimia. But there are lots of other nice benefits too such as gaining additional acceptance and support from your loved one, knowing that someone cares for you and will be there when you need them and best of all - no longer needing to hide your bulimia. Telling someone that you have bulimia means you can finally start being true to yourself.

You may be feeling too ashamed to tell anyone but realize that having bulimia is nothing to be ashamed of as it is not your fault. You did not choose to have bulimia, but you did choose to seek recovery and that takes bravery, courage and strength.

........................................................................................

*"I felt so much shame, but once you quit hiding and starting telling a few key people, the shame goes away. I also realized that even though I thought Bulimia was an ENORMOUS problem, once I started telling people I realized that it didn't feel so big. "- Shanna*

........................................................................................

People will have varying reactions to the news that you have bulimia. Some may be surprised, uncomfortable, confused or worried, others may be very understanding and compassionate. You must keep in mind that no matter how they react it will just be their initial reaction to the news. Try to think of telling someone as a gradual process with many conversations and discussions. It can be helpful to provide them with information, perhaps give them this book to read or maybe write a letter explaining your feelings.

You could tell a friend, your family doctor, a counselor, a therapist, phone an eating disorder helpline or talk to a relative or your partner. It's really all about choosing someone that you feel you can trust and will be most comfortable talking to.

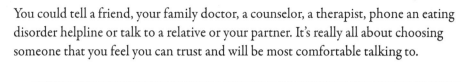

*"I only have one person in my life who knows about my ED history apart from my doctor. It's really a personal decision but if you have someone in your life who you can trust it can be really helpful to have someone to support you like that." - Clara*

If you are uncomfortable confiding in friends or family, seek help online. The Bulimia Help Online Community is full of people who can offer support and understanding.

If you need additional guidance, I recommend working with our Bulimia Help Method Recovery Coaches. Together, your BHM coach can help keep you accountable and consistent in recovery through continued support, guidance and expertise.

A BHM Recovery Coach can help:
- Support you when you fall off track or slip up.
- Troubleshoot solutions to any obstacles in recovery.
- Keep you motivated when you feel disillusioned.
- Answer your recovery questions.
- Help you meal plan.
- Guide you through the Bulimia Help Method.
- Be your rock, foundation and anchor in your recovery.
- Teach you the right mindset along with the habits and behaviors necessary for lifelong recovery.
- Guide you down the path to a full recovery.

All of our Recovery Coaches have suffered from bulimia in their past and more importantly recovered using the Bulimia Help Method. Our coaches have experienced the pain of living with bulimia and the incredible relief, joy and freedom of recovery. They are deeply passionate about your recovery because they are determined for you to experience that freedom from bulimia too. That's why we get the results that we do.

You can learn more about our coaching programs at **www.bulimiahelp.org**

This is a big topic, for further information and for a booklet you can hand to someone after you have told them about your eating disorder go to bulimiahelp.org/bonus and download these two PDF guides:

1. How to tell someone you have bulimia
2. What to do when someone tells you they have bulimia

# I'm Scared To Let Go of Bulimia.

Many sufferers are scared to let go of their bulimia. They believe that their eating disorder is helping them cope with life in some way and once removed life will be much more challenging. Let's dispel some of the common excuses people use to justify their bulimia...

## "Bulimia helps me to manage my emotions"

If bulimia helps you to manage your emotions then you must be blissfully happy and always content. I am guessing not. This is one of the biggest illusions with bulimia. Bulimia doesn't control your emotions, it makes your emotions worse. It wears you down day by day, erodes your confidence, creates anxious thoughts and steals your self-esteem. Without bulimia your emotions will be much more manageable and positive.

## "Bulimia helps me to cope with life"

Is it really helping you to cope? What you are really saying is that it works as a distraction from other problems. These are problems that wouldn't feel so big if you were not bulimic. With bulimia, small challenges can seem so much bigger. The constant stress of dealing with your bulimia only adds a further burden to your life and lowers your natural ability to cope with stress and upset.

## "Bulimia is a comforting friend and it's always there for me"

Only because you believe that bulimia is giving you something in return. Why would you want to be friends with someone who just takes, takes and takes? Bulimia is constantly taking away your pride, self-respect and confidence, and never giving you anything positive back in return.

## "Bulimia gives me control over my life"

If bulimia truly gave you control over your life you would be able to stop binge eating at any time. You would feel in control of your emotions and you food intake. But again I'm guessing that you're not. Bulimia does not give you any control over your life.

## "Bulimia provides a sense of achievement or ownership"

Bulimia is behavioral; it isn't something that you can own. If you are craving a sense of achievement just imagine how accomplished you're going to feel when you recover.

## "It's what I know best and I am scared to change"

It's normal and natural to fear change, especially if we are not sure what benefits change will bring. What if I was to tell you that you have won the lottery and you are now a millionaire? Is this the sort of change you could easily accept? Take note: recovering from bulimia will be so much better than winning the lottery. You will be winning back your self-esteem, confidence, personality, energy, vibrancy, wellbeing and happiness.

Bulimia gives you nothing of benefit, all it does is destroy your life. Bulimia has destroyed your wellbeing, confidence and self-esteem so much that you feel like you can't cope without it. It is bulimia that is making you feel this way. Everyone needs to eat food but no one needs to gorge on huge quantities of it!

Think of it this way...could you convince a non-bulimic to become bulimic? If you had children would you encourage them to be bulimic?

*"Come on kids, it takes your time, energy and health, you will lose your self-esteem, confidence, zest for life, it won't help you lose weight and it may eventually kill you."*

Can you see how detrimental these excuses are and how much of your thinking has been distorted by the bulimia illusion?

*"I always thought bulimia was my crutch. I thought I couldn't cope with life without it. Recovery has taught me that I can cope so much better without bulimia. The idea that bulimia actually helps you to cope with life better is just an illusion, it makes things so much worse. Now I have energy, time, patience and understanding now and I am emotionally stronger than I've ever been." Angela M.*

I understand that this may be difficult to take on board, but for recovery it can really help us when we accept the reality that bulimia gives us nothing. If we wrongly believe bulimia gives us something in recovery we may feel like we are giving up something of value or that we won't be able to cope without it.

## A better way to look at recovery...

Don't look at recovery as though you are giving something up. Instead think of it as gaining everything. You are discovering the amazing person you are without the shackles of bulimia. You are getting your life back.

If you have had bulimia for a long time you may not be sure who you are without bulimia. Like a superhero discovering his powers for the first time, so you to will discover all that you can be once you are free from the kryptonite that is bulimia.

- Your journey will bring thousands of discoveries, with new ones arriving each day.
- You will discover what calm feels like, what balance feels like, what contentment feels like.
- You will discover that you can easily engage in activities that previously struck fear into the deepest recesses of your heart.
- You will discover what it feels like to have an abundance of energy and a lightness of spirit.
- You will discover new interests and new passions.
- You will discover your inner strength and self-reliance.
- You will discover all the amazing fantastic things that make you the truly wonderful, caring, loving, soulful person you already are.

This is an important point. This is who you already are. Yes you are changing, but you are not becoming a different person. Bulimia was holding you back, robbing you of your life and draining your soul. You were born to fly and soar through the sky but bulimia has shackled you to the ground.

........................................................................................

*"Personally bulimia had pretty much become all that I was. I let it define me, it took away my desire to develop my interests and hobbies and basically dominated all areas of my life. The idea of recovery was so intimidating at first because I didn't know who I was going to be at the end of it all, what if I didn't like the real me*

*Slowly my personality started emerging, I started to discover what really made me tick, I began to awaken long lost interests and made new ones too. My relationships improved, I felt more sociable and life became more amazing than I ever thought it could be.*

*I remember this one time sitting with friends just a few months into my own recovery and my friend turns to me and says, "I never realized how funny you were." That moment will stay with me forever, it almost took my breath away. Without bulimia my personality was beginning to awaken and others were noticing it too - there is no feeling quite like that. As bulimia moves out "life" moves in." - Catherine Liberty Recovery Coach*

## Are you ready to get started on your recovery?

I hope so, but just to encourage you a little more I asked some of our readers who have already recovered following this program to share some words of encouragement.

"Never EVER Give up on recovery" - Rachel K
"This program works!!" - Renee Smith
"Have faith in yourself" - Amy L
"You can do this!" - Jessica
"Everyday is an opportunity to advance further in recovery" - Kathryn
"Overcoming bulimia is simply a chance to prove to yourself how strong and capable you really are. Never doubt recovery. You CAN do it!" - Annri
"Take action NOW" - Una
"Believe in yourself. You are wonderful, unique and resourceful" - Olga B
"Who will you be once you're recovered? If you don't stick this out, you'll never get to know!" - Katherine
"This program truly works. Over 20 years of hell to freedom. If you believe........ you CAN :-) You're worth it!!!" - Mary

Let's get started shall we?

# Stage 1 in Recovery: **Structured Eating**

Welcome to stage 1 of recovery "Structured Eating". This is it. This is where we really start to take action to finally remove bulimia from your life once and for all.

The name of the chapter probably gives it away, but this stage is going to be all about learning how to gradually introduce a structured eating program into your daily life. This is the most powerful thing you can do to reduce the urge to binge. By following the steps in this stage you can expect a massive 50% to 90% reduction in your binge urges! So it is essential that you really focus on getting these core elements in place.

The basic principles of structured eating are:
1. Eat three meals and three snacks a day, every day.
2. Eat regularly, leaving no more than 3 hours between meals and snacks.
3. Eat a portion of carbohydrates, fats and protein for each meal.
4. Increase your portion size until you are eating your recommended amount of calories.

Structured eating will help form a solid, stable foundation for the rest of your recovery. Everything else you do in recovery will be built upon these principles.

**Structured eating has many, many benefits and will help to:**

- ✓ Undo the damage of malnutrition.
- ✓ Stop restricting food.
- ✓ Feed your body the nutrition it needs.
- ✓ Rebalance your blood sugar levels.
- ✓ Kickstart your digestive system.
- ✓ Increase your metabolism.
- ✓ Normalize your hunger.
- ✓ Normalize your satiety.
- ✓ Remove your urge to binge on food.
- ✓ Relearn normal eating habits.

What is important to remember is that structured eating is only temporary. This is not the way you are going to eat for life. It's not realistic or healthy for anyone to stay on a meal plan like this forever. Eating cannot (and should not) be "perfect" and inflexible. It can help to think of this early stage as having training wheels on a bicycle. They offer you support when you need them, but after a while when your confidence and ability improves you can get rid of them.

Structured eating is a trial and error process. You can keep adjusting your structured eating plan until you find the right balance you need to stay satisfied and binge-free. From our own experiences and from the feedback we've received from our members, structured eating starts to feel easier after the first month with many saying that they start to appreciate the process of structured eating after the first 2-3 months. Of course, some of us adapt sooner, and others may need a little longer, but this is a general guideline.

You can come back to this stage throughout recovery when you need extra support. When stress hits, when the unexpected happens, when you're feeling weak or when you're fearing a relapse, you can fall back on structured eating to support and stabilize you. We have broken this stage down into steps. Please take one step at a time, and when you feel ready and confident you can move to the next step. Only move at a pace and speed that feels right for you.

........................................................................................

*"When I first began structured eating in January, it was very tough and for the first 4-5 weeks of it, all I thought about was what am I going to have at my next meal? After about 5 weeks of structured eating, it was unlike anything I've ever experienced before. I just didn't think about the next meal! Trust me on this; I've been bulimic for 16 years so I did not think this would happen. If you keep being strong though, and don't give up, even if you have little slip ups, your body will adapt and given a few weeks, your brain will automatically stop thinking like this. I didn't think it would happen either, but it did!" - Laura J*

........................................................................................

**Important Medical Disclaimer:** It is important to have any recovery effort from restrictive eating behaviors overseen by medical professionals. If at anytime during the early phase of recovery you are dizzy, light-headed, feverish, vomit, experience severe swelling of the hands or feet, and/or experience chills and sweats, you need to seek immediate emergency care.

With that being said, let's get started with step 1

# Structured Eating Step 1:
## Begin to eat 'at least' every 3 hours

A lot of bulimics tend to follow a chaotic, disordered eating schedule. They skip meals, they fast for hours and because of this the end of every meal or snack becomes the beginning of an undetermined period of starvation. Physiologically, this encourages a powerful urge to overeat at every opportunity possible.

We need to retrain our mind and body to expect food often and regularly. To do this we need to feed ourselves at least every three hours. By doing this you are telling your body:

........................................................................................

*"You don't have to force me to binge on large amounts of food now because I will provide you with more food later".*

........................................................................................

It will take time for your body to trust that it can have more food later, but if you continue to eat something at least every three hours your body will become biologically reconditioned to know that it will always have access to food.

If you are worried that eating often will lead to weight gain, keep in mind that eating regularly is one of the best things you can do to maintain a healthy weight, as it provides a massive boost to your metabolism.

Studies show that people who skip meals during the day and then eat lots in the evening, tend to be more overweight than those who eat regularly throughout the day. Eating regularly also helps to stabilize your blood sugar levels which will automatically suppress your appetite. And best of all, by eating something at least every three hours you can expect a massive reduction in your binge urges.

## The basic format of eating every 3 hours:

Eat at least three meals and three snacks every day, ensuring you eat (at least) every three hours in the day.

It can help to set your times prior to starting. An example of this would be:

- 8.00am: Breakfast time
- 10.30am: Morning snack
- 1.00pm: Lunch time
- 3.30pm: Afternoon snack
- 6.00pm: Dinner time
- 8.30pm: Evening snack

Meals do not need to be exactly three hours apart. We just need to ensure that there is no more than three hours between meals.

...................................................................................................

*"You have to EAT. I went to therapy for a year and she never told me to eat. Seriously. You must EAT every 3 hours. No questions asked. Period. You choose what to eat, but put food in your body every 3 hours. This was essential for me!" - Shanna*

...................................................................................................


## FAQs

### "When should I start?"
You can start whenever you feel ready. If you are feeling brave, why not start right now? Remember this is going to be a major building block to lifelong recovery, the sooner you start, the better!

### "How rigid should I be with the preset times?"
It is important to stick to your scheduled times, but it is okay to be a little flexible. Some people prefer to eat exactly at their preset time, while others prefer a little flexibility and perhaps eat half an hour either side of their preset times. Feel free to experiment and discover what works best for you.

### "But, what will I eat?"

At this stage don't feel pressured to eat something that will cause anxiety or something you know you will have trouble keeping down. In time, you can introduce more variety, but for now, stay safe and stick to foods you feel comfortable eating. If you know certain foods can trigger a binge then avoid them for now.

### "What if I don't have any foods that I consider safe?"

This can be challenging, but if possible make a list of foods that you consider most tolerable. Put the foods in order with the most tolerable first. Then eat only small portions of your most tolerable foods to get you started. As you progress in recovery continue to go down the list adding more of the foods to your meal plan.

### "What if I am not hungry?"

It doesn't matter. Even if you do not feel hungry, when it is time to eat, then you should try and eat something. At this stage you simply cannot trust your hunger signals. Bulimia has made your internal food regulatory system unreliable. Eating in a mechanical way like this is important until you are able to trust your own hunger and satiety cues.

### "What if I don't feel satisfied after eating?"

In the beginning, expect to have some difficultly feeling satisfied after eating. This is because it takes time for your body to experience and understand feelings of satiety again. Realize that this is very normal and continue with your meal plan.

### "Should I ever listen to my own hunger cues at this stage?"

Generally at the start of recovery you need to focus on eating at least every 3 hours regardless of how hungry you feel. Please don't worry too much about relying on your natural hunger cues just yet; you can learn to be more intuitive as time goes on. Remember it can take 3-6 months and sometimes longer for your natural hunger cues to really start working again.

### "If I can't eat that amount of food, what should I do?"

The goal at this stage is to start getting used to feelings of food in your stomach, so you decide your own portion size. If you are struggling to keep the food down, make your portions smaller. In time, when your body adjusts to regular food, you can increase the amount.

If you find eating three large meals and three snacks too difficult at first, try eating six small meals throughout the day instead. Many find six small meals a lot easier and it's just as effective. Perhaps try it out for a day or two and see if it works better for you.

### "Do I have to eat breakfast?"

I recommend you do eat breakfast. The University of Tasmania (Australia) published a study in the American Journal of Clinical Nutrition which found that both children and adults who skip their morning meal tend to have overall worse eating behaviors and exercise less than those who do eat breakfast. People who skip breakfast also tend to have higher cholesterol, elevated insulin levels, and larger waist circumferences.

A Harvard University study indicated that people who miss breakfast are four times more likely than others to become obese.

Starting the day with a good breakfast breaks that restrictive cycle, helps you to get used to eating earlier in the day and it does wonders to help reduce evening binge urges. If you find it hard to eat breakfast perhaps try getting up a little earlier to give you stomach time to "wake up".

### "Why am I hungrier after eating?"

Unfortunately at this stage in recovery your hunger might not make logical sense. Sometimes eating a meal can make you hungrier than before. Accept that this is another part of your recovery and in time your body will adjust and respond normally to food.

### "What if I binge?"

First of all don't panic; you haven't blown your recovery. At this early stage you are not expected to just instantly stop bingeing. Most people have a tendency to restrict after a binge to try and avoid weight gain, but restriction only leads to more binging later, which is completely counterproductive. If you do binge you need to get back to your structured eating plan as quickly as possible. Please continue your meal plan for the rest of the day. Yes, I know this is challenging but the best way to prevent further binging is to continue to eat at least every three hours.

### "What if I miss a meal?"

If you miss a meal try to eat again as soon as possible. It can be really helpful to carry a couple of healthy snacks with you at all times in case you get caught out. Even if it's just a piece of fruit and a small packet of nuts. Also be wary that you may need to increase your portion size in the next meal to make up for the missed food.

........................................................................................................

*"I found that, after adopting structured eating, I tend to get very anxious when I have to miss a snack or meal. The solution for me was to make sure I always have a small snack at hand e.g. an apple. This definitely takes away some of the stress and not to mention it calms binge urges dramatically!" - Audrey N.*

........................................................................................................

## Summary

It is crucial to begin to eat something at least every three hours during the day. This could be either six small meals or three larger meals and three snacks. Choose foods and portion sizes that you are comfortable eating.

# Structured Eating Step 2:
# Eat Balanced Meals

In their book 'Nutrition Counseling in the Treatment of Eating Disorders' (2012), nutritionists Marcia Herrin and Maria Larkin suggest that each meal (and preferably each snack) should have a combination of all 3 primary macronutrients:

1. A serving of complex carbohydrates.
2. A serving of protein.
3. A serving of fat.

The two main reasons for this are:

1. Bulimics tend to eat the same familiar (safe) foods over and over. Poor nutrition can come partly from the lack of variety in food groups. This, along with constant bingeing and purging can lead to malnourishment and health problems. In order to heal, you need to start eating foods from all food groups to ensure that you are getting the right nutrition for recovery.

2. In addition, a study published in the International Journal of Eating Disorders found that when blood sugar levels were too low, the desire to binge on carbohydrate (sugar) rich foods would intensify. In a separate study, 20 bulimic women were put on a sugar-stabilizing diet to see if it would help with their urges to binge and purge. Within three weeks all of the 20 participants had completely stopped bingeing and all of them remained free from binges in the long term too (Dalvit-McPhillips, 1984).

The solution is to eat regular meals and snacks made up from fats, proteins and complex carbohydrates. This will help to stabilize erratic blood sugar levels and in turn reducing those binge urges.

At this point I do want to stress that I am not a Registered Dietitian. The information provided here is from trusted, qualified, nutritionists and eating disorder specialists but is meant as guidance only. Please see a registered dietitian before undertaking any meal plans.

## Ok, so let's discuss the role of carbohydrates

Carbohydrates provide most of the energy needed in our daily lives, both for normal body functions (such as heartbeat, breathing, digestion, and brain activity) and for exercise (like biking, walking, running up the stairs and all types of resistance training). An ample supply of carbohydrates is absolutely necessary to sustain a healthy existence and a must for bulimia recovery. They also play a critical role in brain health and contribute to serotonin production. Serotonin is the main neurotransmitter regulating your mood and appetite. So when you restrict your intake of carbohydrates you can put yourself at risk of lower serotonin levels, which in turn can affect your mood. *(Wurtman RJ Brain serotonin, carbohydrate-craving, obesity and depression, 1995).*

Types of carbohydrates to add to your meal plan:

- Squash
- Corn
- Sweet potatoes
- Other potatoes
- Brown rice
- Whole grain breads
- Wholemeal bagels
- Whole grain cereals
- Wholemeal pasta
- Legumes
- Fruits and vegetables
- Pumpkin
- Lentils
- Split peas soup
- Oats
- Barley
- 70% cocoa chocolate
- Millet
- Quinoa
- Carob

Aim to get 45 to 65 percent of your daily calories from carbohydrates. Carbohydrates have 4 calories a gram. Based on a 2,000-calorie-a-day diet, this amounts to 900 to 1,300 calories a day, or about 225 to 325 grams (Mayoclinic.org).

## The importance of protein

According to health professionals, protein is essential for bulimia recovery. 'Protein makes you feel fuller for longer by balancing your blood sugar; it modulates your appetite and greatly reduces binge cravings' (Rolls, Hetherington and Burley, 1988). All of which is essential for anyone recovering from an eating disorder.

Ideas for adding protein to your meal plan:
- Eat more legumes (beans) as they have about 7g of protein per serving whereas other whole grains like brown rice and whole wheat bread have 4-5 g protein per serving.
- Eat eggs (including the yolk). Many people stick to eating only egg whites but the egg yolk contains carotenoids, lutein, and vitamin E which can all provide excellent health benefits and disease protection.
- Understand that protein doesn't just have to come from meat. Vegetables, legumes, tofu products, seafood and wholegrains like brown rice, wholegrain pastas and breads are great sources of protein.

..........................................................................................................

*"Protein sources that have been great for me: protein powder in fruit smoothies, hard boiled eggs, cottage cheese, high quality yogurt with lots of probiotics. Homemade jello has protein and can be kind of dessert, too. I use natural gelatin and cook it with organic juice or lemonade. Tofu squares are good. They're firm so they can travel with you and they come in a variety of flavors. Premade protein shakes are kind of icky tasting but have been really great for me on days where I feel in danger of either skipping meals or bingeing." - Tania B*

..........................................................................................................

Aim to get 10 to 35 percent of your total daily calories from protein. Protein has 4 calories a gram. Based on a 2,000-calorie-a-day diet, this amounts to about 200 to 700 calories a day, or about 50 to 175 grams a day (Mayoclinic.org).

## Let's discuss fat

Did you know eating fat helps to curb overeating and can allow you to feel full, content and satisfied after eating? Also, getting a little more of your calories from fat at the start of recovery can also help to reduce that initial bloating that happens within the first few weeks.

It is now increasingly recognized that the "low-fat campaign" has been based on little scientific evidence and may have caused unintended health consequences. While we know that too many saturated and unhealthy fats can be detrimental to health, it is important to remember that healthy fats are vital for health, disease prevention and recovery.

.................................................................................................

*"I used to be terrified of eating anything that contained fat - so whenever I prepared a meal with fat in as part of my structured eating I'd find myself being bombarded with the usual "do not eat this" - "fear this" type-thoughts.  As soon as I recognized those thoughts, I didn't try to bury them or hide from them but I did try to guide them to better places. I accepted I was afraid but then I'd ask myself "what is the fat in this meal really doing?" I'd remind myself that after eating food containing fat I'd experience less binge urges, feel fuller for longer and even absorb all of the other wonderful nutrients from vegetables." Catherine Liberty, Recovery Coach*

.................................................................................................

Ideas for adding fat to your meal plan:
We don't want to get obsessed with healthy and unhealthy fats so rather than thinking about fats that you should limit, try instead to focus on all of those wonderful healthy fats that will help you in recovery.

Here are a few suggestions you can start putting into your diet today:
- Almonds - great to snack on and good source of omega 3.
- Avocados - high in heart-healthy oleic acid.
- Egg yolks - they're rich in omega-3' and contain the full spectrum of amino acids, and have plenty of vitamins your body needs.
- Fish - wild-caught salmon is a great choice, but any fish will do.
- Walnuts - another great choice for snacking.

- Cheese - although dairy may contain more saturated fats it also has a whole range of health benefits. For example 2 servings of dairy per day may reduce your risk of certain cancers.
- Extra virgin olive oil - a great source of vitamin E, Extra virgin olive oil has been related to a decreased risk of coronary heart disease and cancer while having a positive effect on cholesterol levels.
- Nut Butters - peanut butter, cashew butter, almond butter, etc. Nuts and nut butters are a great source of both protein and fat and including them as a part of your snacks can really help you to curb those binge urges!

If you have been avoiding fat, take your time reintroducing it into your diet. Start with small portions and build it up. It may take a while for your digestive system to relearn how to process food.

Aim to get 20 to 35 percent of your daily calories from fat. Fat has 9 calories a gram. Based on a 2,000-calorie-a-day diet, this amounts to about 400 to 700 calories a day, or about 44 to 78 grams of total fat (Mayoclinic.org).

## Fruit and vegetables

Fruit and vegetables in general are healthy, low fat foods. As a result, these tend to be popular safe foods for bulimics. Fruits and vegetables are wonderful foods but they do not provide us with all of the nutrients we need to be healthy. Be careful not to eat too many fruits and vegetables at the expense of other food groups.

## Snacks

Snacks keep blood sugar levels balanced throughout the day and they help manage hunger. Preferably your snacks should be high in complex carbohydrates.

Some snack ideas include:
- Fruit and ricotta cheese.
- Muesli bar.
- A chocolate bar.
- Dried fruit and nuts.
- An apple and a biscuit.
- Cheese and crackers.

## Adding water to your meal plan

Many bulimics are unaware that they are living in a state of chronic dehydration. Purging (as well as using diuretics, laxatives or diet pills) forces a lot of fluids out of the body. Additionally, bulimics tend to consume a lot of caffeine through coffee, tea and diet sodas. Caffeine is a diuretic and increases water excretion.

Water makes up approximately 60% of our body mass and about 80% of our brain. Even slight dehydration (lack of water) can have a significant impact on our daily lives. The effects of dehydration include poor concentration, headaches, impaired sleep, dry skin, joint problems, sore eyes, digestive disorders and kidney problems. Lack of water is the number-one trigger for daytime fatigue. (http://www.nhs.uk)

The best way to remain fully hydrated is to drink water regularly during the day, whether you are thirsty or not. Try increasing your water intake gradually over the next few days and see if you notice any benefits in your wellbeing. Keep in mind that you may want to avoid water at meal times to avoid feeling overly full.

## Some recommended supplements for your meal plan

Due to malnutrition, people with bulimia are much more likely to suffer from vitamin and mineral deficiencies. This can lead to all sorts of problems including anxiety issues, cognitive impairment, depression and can even increase obsessive and compulsive thoughts and lower self-esteem. Here are some supplements you may wish to add to your meal plan, although please consult your doctor before doing so:

### A daily multivitamin

Many people feel the benefits by taking a high quality daily multivitamin, containing the antioxidant vitamins A, C, E, the B-vitamins, and trace minerals, such as magnesium, calcium, zinc, phosphorus, copper and selenium. Make sure the multi-vitamin has a balanced B complex. This has been shown to be good with helping the body cope with stress.

### Zinc

One five-year study, reported by Dr. Schauss, showed an astounding 85% recovery rate for anorexia in patients given zinc supplementation. It concluded: "The zinc supplementation resulted in weight restoration, better body function and improved outlook."

### Omega-3 oils

Omega-3 is not only good for helping ease anxiety and stress; it also has many other reported health benefits, such as lowering blood pressure and possibly reducing the risk of coronary heart disease.

## Other things to think about...

### Calcium

Most bulimics are woefully low in calcium *(Marcia Herrin, 2012)* so you will also want to try to increase your calcium consumption throughout the day. A great way to increase your intake of calcium is to eat vegetables like cabbage, spinach, kale and broccoli since they have many other health benefits in addition to calcium.

### Potassium

Most bulimics are deficient in potassium *(Marcia Herrin, 2012)* which is essential for the proper functioning of the heart, kidneys, muscles, nerves, and digestive system. Some recommended sources of potassium are: coconut water, bananas, oranges, apricots, avocado, potatoes, tomatoes, cucumber, cabbage, tuna, beef, chicken, sardines, and salmon.

## Combining foods to help stabilize blood sugar

Some people find that they experience an increase in binge urges after eating simple carbohydrates due to blood sugar fluctuations but you don't need to fear simple carbohydrates and you don't need to avoid them completely. Simply combining them with foods that contain a source of fat and/or protein can help. This slows down the absorption of glucose into the bloodstream and prevents sugar highs and sugar crashes.

As an example, a typical snack might be banana and a small container of plain greek yogurt, perhaps mixed with Chia seeds for some fiber. Another example would be combining almonds with an apple for slower sugar absorption.

**Download you meal planner template**
Go to **www.bulimiahelp.org/bonus** to download your complimentary Bulimia Help
Meal Planner Template. I recommend you print this off and use it as a guide to help
you organize and plan your meals.

## Summary

I know I have just thrown a lot of information at you in this stage. But all you really
need to keep in mind is that you can eat anything you want as long as it is balanced
with the 3 macronutrients.

By ensuring you have a portion of fat, carbohydrate and protein in each of your meals
(preferably in your snacks too) you help to rebalance blood sugars, provide nutrition
and reduce binge urges.

# Structured Eating Step 3:
# Increase your portion size

It is impossible to stop being bulimic if you don't eat enough food. A great deal of research exists to prove that food cravings are in fact biologically driven as a result of under-eating/low weight. Binges can occur from even gradual, minor under eating over a period of a few days. To fully recover, it is essential to increase your meal portion sizes to ensure you are eating an adequate amount of calories daily. *(Fairburn, CG, Cognitive Behaviour Therapy & Eating Disorders 2008).*

## How much should I be eating?

Although we do not like to discuss calories, the chart below from 'MyPyramid.gov' helps you determine your optimum daily calories. If you restrict a lot, you may be surprised at the amount of calories your body needs.

| Females | Mod Active 30 - 60 daily mins of physical activity. | Active 60+ daily mins of physical activity. |
|---|---|---|
| 19-30 | 2,200 | 2,400 |
| 31-50 | 2,000 | 2,200 |
| 51+ | 1,800 | 2,200 |
| | | |
| Males | | |
| 19-30 | 2,800 | 3,000 |
| 31-50 | 2,600 | 3,000 |
| 51+ | 2,400 | 2,800 |

*Please note that these are approx. daily calories

## FAQs

### "I have to eat how much???"

You may be shocked by these figures. Remember, these are the US government approved guidelines for calorie intake for optimal healthy living. If you have just learned that your body needs about 2200 calories per day and perhaps you are eating around 1000, then you know that you will need to add a significant amount of food to your daily intake in order to curb any binge urges. I personally believe that anything less than 2000 per day isn't usually enough for people in recovery.

### "How fast should I increase my portion size?"

At the start of recovery it's fine to eat portions of food that you feel comfortable with, because when you first start the re-feeding process it can be incredibly difficult to adjust to eating "normal amounts." But you should be aware that if you take things too slowly then you will find the whole process of recovery much more difficult in the long run. So, the sooner you can start eating a healthy amount of food each day, the better!

From my experience I have noticed the people we coach who seemed to suffer the most weight fluctuations are actually the ones who continue restricting their food. I know that sounds crazy, but scientifically and biologically it makes sense. Not eating enough food lowers your metabolic rate, which in turn teaches your body to store more of the food you eat as fat, rather than allowing you to expend it as energy.

Over the next few weeks gradually increase the size of your portions until you are eating around the recommended calorie amount for your age, height and activity level. After a few weeks if you are still regularly bingeing then you may need to increase the amount you are eating with each meal as this is usually a sign that you are not getting enough food.

### "I am scared to increase my portion size!"

I know this can be scary, but in this step you are tackling food restriction head on. You are really getting to the core of the problem. You can expect big positive changes. You will notice a dramatic reduction in your binge urges, food obsession and anxious thoughts and a big increase in your energy levels, general wellbeing and self-esteem.

*"In the past, before starting recovery if I ever ate more than 500 calories a day I'd see the number on the scale increasing. So when I came here and was told I needed to eat around 2200 calories a day I was beyond terrified. I remember thinking it would be impossible for me, but luckily I was so desperate for recovery I knew I had to try. Sure there were weight fluctuations at first, but eventually things did balance out, I didn't continue to gain weight once my body got used to regular food again."*
Catherine Liberty, Recovery Coach

## "Should I measure my food portions?"

If you wish to measure portions, you can. If you feel that you need to count calories to avoid a binge, you can do that too. Another option is to purchase individual portions from the supermarket (be careful they are the correct size; a lot of the serving sizes in these products are much too small). Also, you can go to a restaurant that serves normal food portions if you don't feel like measuring portions.

Ultimately you don't have to measure anything because dieting, strict portion sizes and counting calories never work in the long run. It's okay for now because you are just starting out but over time you should start to practice setting your own portion sizes. Also be careful when measuring food and counting calories because it can be a slippery slope toward obsession. Try counting and measuring only if you need to for now, and make it a point to stop once you have an understanding of what portion sizes are appropriate for you.

## Getting the balance right

It can be challenging to get the balance right between eating enough so you don't get too hungry and eating too much so you risk feeling the need to purge. If you tend to eat to the point of feeling too full, try taking small breaks during the meal and asking yourself when you should stop. This may take some practice, so be patient with yourself while you figure out appropriate portion sizes.

## Are you eating enough?

In our coaching program we had a woman who was a semi-professional athlete. We tried several approaches and still couldn't understand why her binge urges were so powerful. That was until one day when she realized that because of how active she was in her training and at work, she actually needed more like 4000 calories a day! Pretty extreme case I know, but it is definitely worth considering whether you're eating enough food through the day. If you need help I strongly recommend you discuss your needs with a dietician.

A handy trick to ensure you are eating enough calories is to eat nutrient dense foods for snacks. Perhaps a combination of things like nuts, seeds and nut butters. They won't make you feel overly full but offer a really easy way to meet your calorie and nutrient needs.

...........................................................................................

*"I was at a healthy BMI, and eating regularly, but still restricting at about 1700 calories a day. My weight had plateaued - I was in starvation mode. I had lanugo and malnutrition ridges in my nails. I had no energy and was constantly miserable. Then I upped my intake. Even though I had no weight to gain, I started eating 2500+ calories. After just a week of eating this way, my period came back, my nails started growing normally... I had so much energy!!! I was truly happy. I gained a little initially, but that's all coming off again now. I'm eating plenty, and healthily - but still having treats like custard and chocolate and pizza, some every day. I'm conquering fear foods, and I'm just so much happier. I'm not in quasi anymore. I'm really recovering. And you can do it to. EAT.'" - Lets Recover*

...........................................................................................

*"I wish I could give you all a look inside my head so you could see how wonderful life without bulimia is. You are so much more than this, all of you! But you will never, ever, recover while you are still restricting. You have to put trust in something your disorder does not want you to believe, it is the only way out but god is it worth it." - Debbie F*

...........................................................................................

## Summary

Over the next few weeks gradually increase the size of your meal portions until you are eating around the recommended calorie amount for your age, height, activity level and body type. Give your body time to adjust. You don't want to feel uncomfortably full and risk purging.

# Common Challenges:
# "I don't know what to eat!"

You can eat anything as long as it is balanced with the 3 macronutrients and is a reasonable portion size. I would recommend investing in a good cook book, one that appeals to you. If you do feel that you need more in-depth advice then a physician or a registered dietitian who is familiar with eating disorders can help you to determine your unique caloric needs.

To help you get started, here are some sample meal ideas that adhere to the structured eating principles.

### Breakfast Ideas
- A bowl of porridge with a sprinkle of seed mix (e.g. sunflower, or sesame and pumpkin).
- Cereal with milk or yoghurt and fruit (e.g. banana for potassium).
- Wholemeal/multigrain toast (x2) with jam or marmalade, yoghurt and fruit juice.
- Wholegrain toast (x2) or roll with 2 eggs (poached, scrambled or boiled)
- An egg & a rasher of bacon, plus fruit or juice.
- Turkey rashers fried in a little olive oil with mushrooms and tomatoes.
- Baked beans and toasted wholemeal pitta plus 1/2 grapefruit.
- A pancake: 1 egg, a little milk and oat bran mixed together with a fork, fry in a little olive oil.

### Lunch Ideas
- Thick soup such as chicken and vegetable or bean and vegetable with a bread roll or some toast.
- Bowl of salad with a small tin of tuna and nuts mixed in to it plus a serving of potato/pasta/ couscous/ tabbouleh /salad (to provide carbohydrate & protein).
- Sandwich on wholegrain bread or roll with a slice of meat (or an egg), cheese and salad (tomato, lettuce, cucumber, carrot).
- 1-2 apples diced, topped with cottage cheese and sprinkled with chopped brazil nuts. Serve with a large mixed green leaf salad decorated with curls of smoked salmon and salad dressing.

## Dinner Ideas

- Pasta with a tomato based sauce (include tuna or bacon etc.) served with green vegetables (e.g. broccoli, beans, asparagus) or salad.
- Fish/beef/pork/lamb/chicken with salad or vegetables and potato/sweet potato/pumpkin.
- Stir fried meat/tofu and vegetables with rice or noodles.
- Salmon steak baked in tinfoil parcel with green beans, almond slivers, garlic/onion to taste. Served on bed of quinoa cooked in bouillon(stock).

## Snack Ideas

- Muesli bar.
- A chocolate bar.
- Dried fruit and nuts.
- An apple and a biscuit.
- Cheese and crackers.
- Fruit and ricotta cheese.

# Common Challenges:
# "What's With All The Bloating?"

Let's gets this clear now. Everyone experiences bloating at the start of recovery and it's absolutely 100% perfectly natural, normal and to be expected. When you've suffered with bulimia for a very long time your body stops digesting food properly, your basic metabolic rate lowers and everything really just slows down. On top of this the food that you eat can sit in your digestive tract for longer than normal at first, adding to that initial bloating, gas and discomfort.

Let's take a look at what Dr Wayne Callaway, an Eating Disorders Specialist and Associate Clinical Professor of Medicine at George Washington University had to say about bloating in the early stages of eating disorder recovery:

...................................................................................................

*"When you start to re-feed your body there are a lot of complex reasons why you retain more fluid for a time. For example when you start to digest more carbohydrates your body is forced to produce more insulin, which causes your kidneys to retain salt and water. This increases the permeability, or "leakiness," of the capillaries which can result in a collection of fluid in the spaces between your cells. One of the best ways to reduce initial bloating is to eat more fat, in fact when fluid retention is a problem during the recovery phase, it doesn't hurt to get even more than the RDA of calories from fat to start with." - Dr Wayne Callaway.*

...................................................................................................

### "How long does bloating last?"
Your body will "catch up" sooner than you think. Generally when you first start recovering you should expect your bloating to last anywhere between 2-6 weeks, although a small number of people may experience bloating for a little longer than this. Sometimes you may also notice an increase in the swelling of your parotid glands, but this is very temporary.

### "Is recovery bloating dangerous?"
It's important to understand that while this bloating may feel uncomfortable or even painful it's not dangerous because all you are doing is re-learning how to do something

that is completely natural and safe, which is eating and digesting food. However if you do experience intense, prolonged pain, discomfort or bloating that becomes worrying you should always consult your doctor.

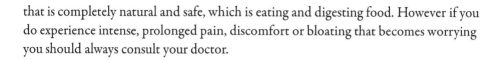

*"I loved discovering the Bulimia Help Method as it really made me believe full recovery was possible for anyone. However the first 6 months of my recovery I put on 15 kilos and developed a very bad acidity problem. I had a wonderful coach who said lots of encouraging things each week but the physical symptoms were not going away.*

*It was only after doing a specialized blood test I realized I had certain intolerances and cut them out of the majority of my meals that my weight normalized and acidity went away. Whilst I know bloating and discomfort is a necessary stage of recovery prolonged discomfort shouldn't be so I think all should be aware of the additional steps you may need to explore"* - Kimberly

### "But I am scared!"

The truth is bloating isn't that bad. Yes it's uncomfortable and annoying but these problems are magnified tenfold because of the FEAR it induces. Let's be honest, if you're not ready for it, bloating can be very scary. Just about everyone can deal with a little discomfort but most people find it difficult to deal with any fear. Fear is an extremely powerful force and this is why bloating causes so many people to quit recovery.

Here are some of the fear thoughts you may experience:
- You may have fear that it's not bloating but fat.
- You may fear that what you're experiencing is abnormal.
- You may fear that your bloating is too extreme.
- You may fear that you have developed food intolerances.
- You may fear that your bloating will never go away and that your body will never be able to adjust.
- You may fear that there is something seriously wrong with you and you can never recover.

These fear thoughts can run through your mind all day long. This is to be expected. It is okay to be a scared here. You are facing your fears, of course you are going to be a little paranoid and worried. Understand that this is all part of the recovery process. Being scared and worried about bloating is a normal, expected, typical step in the recovery process. So please don't let it force you to give up on your recovery.

The truth is there is no need to panic at all. Keep in mind that most of these fear thoughts have no basis in reality because they are fears, not facts. Your body can handle the food. A bloated stomach is not a fatter stomach, it's a healing stomach. Food in your stomach is not fat. Bloating will not turn to fat. In time the bloating will pass. Please, please, please be patient with your body and give it time to heal. A lifetime free from bulimia far outweighs a couple of weeks worth of feeling bloated.

..........................................................................................................

*"I had not eaten and digested a proper meal in probably 5 or so years so my body freaked out a bit when I first started eating meals. That feeling of having food in my belly would just flick me into binge mode as my body was so used to being stuffed with food whenever that feeling came. Sitting through that feeling was so difficult.*

*The best thing to do for me was to eat lots of small meals each day so it would feel more comfortable. I still would feel bloated by the end of the day but each day gets easier, the more food you allow your body to digest the better it gets at it. After a week I noticed a huge improvement and finally now at almost a month I feel like my digestion is almost back to normal! I am so proud of my body for learning so quickly!" - Shannon*

..........................................................................................................

**Some great tips to help with bloating**
Many people find that they go up a dress size or two during the bloating phase of recovery, and the weight fluctuations that follow can mean that your clothing size is a little unpredictable for the first few months. If this happens please try your best to remain calm and to embrace the journey. It is a temporary struggle that will lead you to a lifetime of freedom. If you can, invest in some comfortable, loose fitting clothing to help yourself through this phase of recovery. Avoid tight fitting waistbands and instead find styles that make you feel beautiful and less body-conscious.

**Other tips to deal with bloating include:**

- Sip water throughout the day to prevent excess water retention.
- Try eating 6 small meals rather than 3 large meals and snacks.
- Try eating foods with fat present. You need to eat fewer of them to feel satisfied
- Try herbal teas such as peppermint tea, dandelion tea, ginger tea, but please avoid 'laxative' teas.
- Avoid excess salt
- Walking and light exercise can help to get your intestinal muscles working again and it will generate bowel movement.
- Try to avoid taking diuretics or 'water pills' as they can make bloating worse in the long run.

**Before we move forward...**

Really, there is no point moving forward in this program unless you can answer "yes" to the following question. Are you willing to experience a short period of bloating in order to live the life your truly deserve free from the shackles of bulimia?

I know it's scary, but I'm hoping the answer is a loud and clear YES!

# Common Challenges:
## Continual Bingeing in Recovery

"I'll never binge again" or "this stops from tomorrow". How many times have you made that promise to yourself during recovery?

In truth promising yourself that you will never binge again isn't a great idea. It just sets yourself up for failure. It pushes you to seek a 'perfect' recovery, which does not exist. Then, when you do binge again, you are crushed and convinced that you have failed in recovery even though nothing could be further from the truth.

When starting recovery, you are not expected to just stop bingeing. It takes time for your body to biologically rebalance and the damage caused by malnutrition to fully heal. In some ways the binge urge is testing you, it is making sure you are truly going to give your body the proper nutrition it needs before it trusts you enough to really let go. Gradually you will notice a big reduction in your binge urge, but you must give it time. For some of you it may take 3-6 months before the binge urge really dissipates. The point is, you can still progress in this recovery program even if you are still bingeing sometimes because it does not mean you are failing!

# Common Challenges:
## Dealing with hunger in between meals

If you find yourself hungry between meals, then the first thing to address is whether you are eating enough food. Most people find the urge to eat between meals can reduce dramatically once they increase their portion size and begin eating foods from all of the major food groups.

Another thing to bear in mind is that in the early stages of recovery it's normal to feel false hunger or emotional hunger between meals. Emotional hunger is very different from physical hunger and it is important that you recognize the difference.

### Non-physical hunger (or emotional hunger)
- Develops suddenly
- Starts above the neck
- Can start at anytime
- Persists despite fullness after eating

### Physical hunger
- Builds up gradually
- Starts below the neck
- Occurs several hours after eating
- Goes away when you are full
- Eating leads to satiety.

### Is it false hunger?
Think about how your hunger feels. Is it a continual urge to eat that is causing you anxiety or panic? Are you having thoughts about eating because you simply can't stop thinking about food and know eating will provide momentary relief? Do you feel hunger above the neck? Do you feel agitated? If so then there is a good chance the hunger you are feeling is not real. Practice accepting these thoughts and feelings and remind yourself calmly that soon it will be time to eat again.

### Is it real hunger?

Is there a rumbling in your stomach? Do you feel faint, weak or lightheaded? Do you think that this is real hunger? Eating every 3 hours is something that does really work for recovery, so rather than starting to snack in-between meals and disrupting this cycle, the best advice is to eat a little more for your meals and snacks.

## Foods that help to remove hunger

If you find yourself hungry between meals try adding a few of these foods:

- **Bananas:** Bananas are a great snack and a great way to nourish your body.
- **Eggs:** Eggs are an excellent source of protein and will keep you full longer.
- **Almonds:** Almonds are rich in monounsaturated fatty acids and protein. Just one handful of almonds will help keep you full.
- **Avocados:** Avocados contain good fats (monounsaturated fatty acids) and protein that will fill you up nicely. Not only can you add avocados to salads, but they are great as a spread on sandwiches and you can even add them to a smoothie.
- **Peanut butter:** Peanut butter is full of protein and a great source of monounsaturated fats.
- **Oatmeal:** Oatmeal is under-appreciated in my opinion. Oatmeal is a great super food because it's low in sugar, high in fiber and it's so quick to prepare. It only takes 5-10 minutes to prepare your oatmeal and you'll be full for hours after eating a bowl.

### "But I feel I am already eating enough!"

Are you sure? Think about this very carefully for a second:

- Do you live a very active lifestyle?
- Do you work long hours or rush around a lot?
- Do you exercise regularly?

If you've answered yes to any of these questions then there is a good chance that your body needs more fuel. When referring to the calorie guidelines make sure that you consider all physical activity (not just driven exercise or work-out times).

### "I'm definitely eating enough, but I still feel hungry in between meals and snacks"

If you are sure you're getting enough calories and that you're eating regularly then it helps to consider the types of foods that you're eating. Have you been following the basic guidelines of including at least one portion of carbohydrate, fat and protein in each meal? Fat and protein helps to slow down digestion which stabilizes blood sugar levels and keeps you fuller for longer.

### "I'm following all of this advice but still feel hungry between meals and snacks!"

If you are continuing to feel hungry at this stage and believe the hunger is real then it does make sense to slightly reduce the time between meals and snacks. Try eating every 2 ½ hours and see if it makes a difference.

### "But I thought recovery was about listening to my hunger not ignoring it?"

You're right, and in time you will learn how to trust your intuitive hunger signals. But right now you can't trust your natural hunger and satiety signals because constant bingeing and purging de-sensitises you to them. Structured eating is a gateway to intuitive eating and offers the best solution for the time being.

### Be careful of continual snacking

In general it's best to avoid continual snacking in between meals. It doesn't help you to learn normal eating patterns and you're probably going to be eating for a mixture of hunger and emotion which is not so great. So it's better to teach yourself how to eat regularly, but not constantly, in order to normalize your eating patterns.

# Common Challenges:
# The Menstrual Cycle

Most women tend to experience an upsurge in binge urges and cravings for sugary, energy dense foods in the days leading up to their period. However, as scary as this can be, research shows that there is a very straightforward explanation; your body simply needs the extra fuel at this time.

Obviously we tend to equate cravings for energy dense foods with bulimia, but again this is your body's way of telling you it needs more food. Try allowing yourself an extra snack or slightly more food at meal times during the lead up to menstruation and know that it is okay to eat the foods you are craving. Also, please understand that there is no need to fear eating more at this time because you'll also experience a small rise in metabolism that compensates for the additional food you have eaten.

Many women experience moodiness and bloating along with menstruation which can also make recovery extra challenging during that time. Be sure and practice extra self-care during this time, and try to rest a little more than usual. Your body is working very hard to go through the process of menstruation, so it deserves some relaxation.

............................................................................................

*"I prepared myself mentally by accepting that those times were going to come and I think this can be one of the most important steps to take, you have to be emotionally ready. I wasn't always able to pinpoint the exact day and time where I'd suddenly feel this frightening increase in hunger or random appearance of binge urges, but I could usually guess accurately within a couple of days. So when that hunger did hit I was waiting for it, expecting it and accepting it as a natural part of my life."*
*- Catherine Liberty, Recovery Coach*

............................................................................................

# Common Challenges:
# Alcohol, Caffeine, and Drugs

## Alcohol

Alcohol hinders recovery for three common reasons. The first is that it lowers your inhibitions and can cause you to care less about your recovery. This inability to think clearly can lead you to abandon your progress and binge. The second reason it is harmful is because our bodies process alcohol as sugar. A sudden spike in sugar leads to a sugar crash afterwards. This can create a binge urge or encourage more drinking. The third reason alcohol hinders recovery is that alcohol leads to dehydration. Your body is working hard now to heal and become balanced. Staying hydrated is a big part of that healing process. If you wake up dehydrated from drinking, you may be more likely to binge.

Alcohol is a massive trigger for bulimic urges so if you cannot drink moderately (a maximum of 1 alcoholic drink daily), do not drink at all while you are trying to establish a regular pattern of eating. If you have a drinking problem I recommend you try to resolve that issue before tackling your eating disorder. I have heard great reviews about the book 'The Easy Way to Stop Drinking' by Allen Carr. Alternatively you may wish to visit your doctor or local community alcohol support service for further advice.

## Caffeine

Be smart with caffeine. Bulimics tend to drink a lot of diet sodas, coffees and tea to keep going but this is no substitute for food energy. Excessive caffeine raises stress hormone levels, increases anxiety and interferes with sleep quality. Cut out coffee for a week (perhaps drink de-caffeinated) and see how you feel. After you get over the initial withdrawal symptoms you should feel more calm, rested and less sensitive to emotional binge urges.

## Recreational Drugs

It makes sense to refrain from all illegal drugs. Not only do they seriously harm your health and quality of life but they can also dramatically alter your mood and impact on your ability to remain rational. They could seriously jeopardize your ability to stick with recovery for the long term. Bulimia has long been associated with comorbid substance abuse. If you are suffering from drug addiction and are not able to 'just stop' taking drugs I urge you to seek treatment as soon as you possibly can. As a first step you can visit your doctor or access details of treatment services online.

# Helpful Tools for Structured Eating

Here are some tools to help you with structured eating. These are purely optional, but I recommend you give a few of them a go and see what works best for you.

# Mental Rehearsal

Eating out with others, parties, family dinners and seasonal celebrations can all pose a challenge to your recovery. Try using mental rehearsal to help yourself overcome these challenging situations. Mental rehearsal works on the simple principle that your nervous system cannot tell the difference between a real or vividly imagined thought. So when you imagine performing a situation, you are in a way training your brain to perform this way in real life. This process isn't intended to build unrealistic expectations; it is simply designed to improve your readiness for the real situation.

### How to use mental rehearsal
- This doesn't have to take long at all, just close your eyes and take a few minutes to visualize the upcoming meal.
- Imagine yourself acting confidently, feeling happy and making food choices that are recovery-friendly.
- Imagine the food on your plate, delicious, not too little and not too much.
- Imagine yourself feeling content throughout your meal and peaceful at the end with no urges to continue eating no matter how delicious it all was.
- Imagine yourself dealing with any bulimic urges in a calm and recovery-focused manner. You are accepting them without allowing them to knock you off balance.
- Imagine yourself dealing with others in a peaceful and calm way too. See yourself no longer feeling triggered in this environment.

Give it a go and see if it makes those specific meal scenarios a little more manageable. You may be surprised by just how powerful this exercise can be.

# Food Journal

You may find that your binge urges become overwhelming on certain days, at specific times of the month, after eating certain foods or when you're around particular people. A food journal can help you to identify these patterns and troubleshoot your recovery. Knowing your personal triggers can help you to plan and prepare for them.

Some people love to journal food intake and others don't. If you find it helpful, I would recommend that you do it. If however you would prefer not to, or don't think it will be helpful, then it's fine not to keep a food journal.

### What to food journal
- To get started I recommend that you track your food intake for just 3 consecutive days each week.
- For three days this week (or more if you would like) your goal is to record everything you eat and drink – while also including some brief notes on how you're feeling at the time.
- Don't worry about recording calories, instead focus more on the type of foods, your feelings of hunger and satiety and your emotional state at the time. Also focus on the physical feelings, are you bloated afterwards? Do you experience reflux? Do you feel uncomfortably hungry?
- At the end of the week, review your food journal and see if you can identify any relationship between the foods that you ate or how regularly you ate and the emergence of binge urges.

# The Daily Check-in

The "Daily Check-in" helps you to refine your recovery plan, reaffirms your current goals and provides a time when you can focus on yourself. It takes around 10 minutes and will be exceptionally beneficial to your recovery.

What to do:
Every day set aside 10 minutes to write in your journal. Try to establish the same set time each day so this becomes a habit.
Answer these three questions:
- Did my recovery go as planned today?
- What impediments, if any, were there to my recovery?
- What can I do to remove these impediments next time?

Write down what you're going to do differently, focus on how you'll overcome the barriers to your recovery and outline some new steps that you can take in the future. Then use this new process the next time an impediment comes up.

You may also wish to jot down your feelings, your energy levels and any changes or insights you noticed during your recovery. Repeat this exercise daily and give it a try for at least two weeks to see how it goes.

## The Weekly Review

As well as daily reviews you can also do a longer weekly review.

What to do:
Choose a single day each week for a more in-depth weekly review. On your weekly review day please record:
- What you learned this week.
- The best things that happened this week.
- Your biggest challenges this week.
- Things you did for the first time.
- Your top three priorities for the week ahead.

This will help you gain more insight and knowledge from the previous week and it can really be helpful for recovery.

# Structured Eating:
## Super Short Version

If you need a quick reminder of what you need to do, here is the super short version of structured eating. Whatever you do just ensure you are sticking to these core principles.

The four basic principles of structured eating are:

- Eat three meals and three snacks a day, every day.
- Eat regularly, leaving no more than 3 hours between meals and snacks.
- Eat at least one portion of carbohydrate, fat and protein for each meal.
- Continue to increase your portion size until you are eating your recommended amount of calories.

Don't forget you can go to **www.bulimiahelp.org/bonus** to download your complimentary Bulimia Help Meal Planner Template. You can print this off and use it as a guide to help you organize and plan your meals.

*"I've reached my 6th day of eating every day, on an average of 3 sensible meals and snacks, and not purging. For someone who, up to 7 days ago, purged everything they ate for the last 11 years, that's a massive thing. Yet because of my secrecy and desperation to seem 'normal', no one really knows about my daily battle of bulimia. It may not seem a very big deal to anyone else, but I know you'll agree that this is a massive achievement and I feel tearful, ecstatic, scared, proud, and anxious all in one go." - Reeva A*

# Marcy's Success Story

"I had bulimia for nineteen horrible years. I just turned 40 this year, and sometimes it's so hard for me to imagine that I have spent almost half my life being bulimic. Before recovering, I had never experienced adulthood without bulimia!

I had always been a kind of chubby kid. I ate a lot to deal with sadness. I was born with a port wine stain on half my face. Boys didn't like me and I got made fun of a lot as a kid. Around the time I turned 16, I decided to go on a diet.

I lost a considerable amount of weight, and discovered that some people would overlook my face if I wasn't fat. I maintained that weight for several years by restricting my diet and doing tons of exercises. A few years later I got married. I was married for ten years and had two daughters.

It was during my first pregnancy that I developed bulimia. I was so intensely hungry, (I now realize it was due to the horrible diet I had been on for so long!). But during my pregnancy I gained a ton of weight and my doctor wasn't very sympathetic. I was told I couldn't gain any more weight and that it was ridiculous for me to have gained so much in the first place. So I felt pressured to take control of my weight.

One night I was sooo hungry, so I ate. I actually got nauseous and sick. Somewhere, somehow, it occurred to me that if I threw up every once in a while, it would help keep my weight down and keep my doctor from yelling at me. I didn't even know anything about bulimia– that's something that I wonder about all the time. Where does that idea come from?

In any case, it spiraled out of control. I tried to get it under control as the years went by, but it was a problem that I hid until 1996. I was able to hide it pretty well, and not many people suspected it. Then something happened that totally blew all my control.

Both of my daughters were killed in separate accidents. My youngest, at three months old, was killed in 96. My oldest was killed in 2001, just shy of her ninth birthday. As you can imagine, my whole world fell apart. My marriage didn't survive it. By 2002 I found myself divorced and alone and my battle with bulimia became a whole different ball game. I binged on everything. 6-8 times a day.

All my money went down the toilet. My health got very bad, very quickly. I held onto some kind of survival until 2010, can you believe that? I still worked, but all my money after paying rent went on food.

I tried everything I could think of to recover. I've been in therapy, tried online programs, tried OA. I was in the hospital shortly after my oldest daughter passed away and they actually did put me in the eating disorders ward. But even the inpatient CBT (cognitive behavioral therapy) didn't stop me. My kidneys started to shut down and my doctor told me I would need dialysis if my bulimia continued.

In any case, I was surfing the net one day and happened upon the Bulimiahelp.org. What the heck, I thought. I have tried everything else, let's give this a shot. I read the book- Wow! For the first time in my life, I was told I am not a mental case! There is something very defeating in being told you have a mental illness. It takes away your confidence in yourself, you just write yourself off as a basket-case. But the Bulimia Help Method told me I was ok!

For the first time I was able to see the connection between that first fateful diet I did way back as a teenager and my battle with bulimia. Are you serious, I said to myself...my diet caused all this?

As I read through the book, it started to sink into my head that maybe, just maybe, it was right. Maybe I could recover. Was it truly as simple as feeding my body the correct things, of letting go of my restriction? I decided to give it a go, to trust the book and give it a chance. That was just over a year ago.

I have had tremendous success with it. I truly cannot express how much of a lifesaver the program has been for me. After years of being told I was mentally ill and that I would never recover, it was a breath of fresh air to find a program that said, no, you CAN recover.

I sit here now, and I can't believe I have energy. I can't believe my face isn't bloated. I can't believe I am strong! I'm amazed at how my body has forgiven me and is healing. As time goes on I thank god every day that I happened to come across the Bulimia Help Method. It worked when nothing else did."


- Marcy

..........................................................................................................

# Stage 2 in Recovery: Stop Bingeing and Purging

Well done, you have now reached stage 2 of the Bulimia Help Method! I'm so glad that you're still here with me on our journey to recovery together.

No matter what's happening in your recovery right now, no matter how far you have left to travel, and no matter how many times you have fallen, if you're here reading these words then it is obvious that you are committed to your recovery. That commitment and determination to recover will carry you through to a life free from bulimia. I want you to know that no matter how unsure you may be feeling, you are stronger than you know. **You can do this!**

Before we begin to explore the strategies that will help you to stop bingeing and purging, I need to stress that in order for these strategies to be effective, you must first implement the principles of structured eating. You must first and foremost feed your body the nutrition it needs. In saying that, it's okay to begin working on this stage while also working on your structured eating plan.

When starting recovery, you are not expected to just stop bingeing. It will take time for your body to biologically rebalance and the damage caused by malnutrition to fully heal. In some ways the binge urge is testing you, it is making sure that you are truly going to give your body the proper nutrition it needs before it trusts you enough to really let go. Gradually you will notice a big reduction in your binge urge, but you must give it time. For some of you it may take 3-6 months before the binge urge really dissipates.

Plus, there may still be another component to your binge urges. Even when you've restored balance to your body, you may still experience what I call 'Emotional Binge Urges'. This is especially true if you have had bulimia for a long time. This is a strong desire to eat food, not for hunger, but to dull negative thought processes and numb any emotional pain.

Some of the conditions that may trigger these kinds of binge urges (among other things) include:
- Stress/anxiety
- Sadness/loneliness/depression
- Frustration/anger
- Cravings
- Self hatred
- Insecurity
- Jealousy
- Feeling overwhelmed
- Fear
- Disappointment
- Irritation with someone
- Feelings of helplessness
- Feeling rushed
- Feeling embarrassed
- Feeling the loss of something
- Resentment
- Complaining
- Feelings of unfairness.

You can see the wide range of suffering. But actually, it's all really the same thing: wishing things were different than they are. An easy way for us to (temporarily) change how we feel about a situation is to comfort ourselves with food. We suffer, so to ease this suffering we binge on food to quiet the mind or to eliminate any uncomfortable feelings.

The process normally goes like this:

- There is a trigger. Something happens that you don't want to happen, (e.g. someone treats you badly).
- You get upset, or suffer in some other way.
- Your conditioning kicks in and you experience an urge to binge on food to numb the feelings.
- To remove the binge urge, you binge on food.

A study published in the Journal of Appetite explored the connection between the experience of negative emotions and neural response to anticipated food intake in individuals with bulimia. They found that as negative emotions increased, so too did responsivity of the brains reward regions.

The individuals with bulimia showed more brain activity when anticipating food than non-bulimics did and this caused researchers to hypothesise that people with bulimia may find it more difficult to resist tempting food cues when in a negative mood. (Bohon & Stice, 2012).

This means that you may be subconsciously conditioned to experience stronger cravings for food when you encounter negative emotions, (especially if you've had an eating disorder for a long time).

Research shows that eating certain foods, especially those with high sugar and fat combinations (e.g. ice cream, chocolate, doughnuts, cakes and pies) produce "feel good" chemicals like serotonin and other endorphins in our brains. Endorphins are powerful, natural opiates that allow you to experience pleasure, a reduction in pain and lower levels of stress. Bingeing on food causes a flood of endorphins to surge through your brain which can temporarily infuse you with a sense of numbness or euphoria. This is extremely similar to drug addiction and makes bingeing highly habit forming. If you've ever experienced that trance-like state during an episode of bulimia, or felt "high" afterwards, then you can point the finger at this endorphin rush. Unfortunately, for those who binge, studies show that despite those temporary highs, the feelings of disgust and self-hatred associated with binge eating completely cancel out any positive effects.

The first time that you binged on food it was mostly likely due to starvation and malnutrition (the physical binge urge). But then as the cycle of binge eating continued, your brain learned that bingeing on food provided a temporary release from uncomfortable emotions and feelings. As a result of this you gradually became conditioned to crave food in response to uncomfortable conditions and negative emotions, (I call this the emotional binge urge). This craving comes from the unthinking part of your brain that reacts automatically based on instincts and habit, rather than logic and reason.

This is similar to smokers who craves a cigarette when they feel stressed, or the drinker who craves alcohol to calm their nerves. They were not born with this desire, but over time their brain has became conditioned to crave cigarettes or alcohol under certain conditions.

Did you know that when someone quits smoking all the physical side-effects of quitting pass within a few days? Yet an ex-smoker can continue to have strong cravings, pangs and longings for a cigarette for weeks and even months after quitting. The reason for these cravings has nothing to do with physical addiction and everything to do with habit and conditioning. Over time, as the conditioning fades, so too do the cravings.

### What is the difference between Emotional Binge Urges and Physical Binge Urges?

An Emotional Binge Urge usually starts above the neck, it is a craving to eat food for emotional comfort and to escape from unpleasant feelings. A Physical Binge Urge usually starts below the neck, it is a primal drive to eat food which is triggered by malnutrition and food restriction.

### Should I focus on removing my Emotional Binge Urges first?

No. It is absolutely essential that you address the Physical Binge Urges first through a structured eating plan. Once your Physical Binge Urges have been resolved you will notice a vast improvement in your emotional well-being and at that point it will be much easier to overcome any Emotional Binge Urges that may remain.

## Are my emotions to blame for my binge urges?

The mainstream view of bulimia today is that bulimics binge to cope with negative thoughts, feelings and circumstances.

I disagree.

Spend a moment imagining this scenario: Something happens in your day that triggers an uncomfortable emotion, for example someone is extremely rude to you at the grocery store. This makes you feel insecure and depressed. Normally these emotions would trigger an urge to binge but the strange thing is - you have no urge to binge at all. None what so ever. You still feel the uncomfortable emotion, but now there is no urge to eat food. Now the question is... Would you still binge on food to deal with the uncomfortable emotion even though you had no urge to do so?

I am guessing not. That would be like smoking a cigarette to help calm your nerves even though you have no desire to do so.

Emotions alone do not make you want to binge, it's only when they are connected with the subconscious, automatic, conditioning that you experience the "urge to binge".

Yes, negative emotions may trigger a binge urge, but they are not responsible for the urge. Non-bulimics who are perfectly healthy still experience negative thoughts and feelings, yet they do not experience any binge urges to dull these feelings. This is because their brains have not been conditioned to do so.

Blame the conditioning, not the emotions. If we blame our emotions, then this can lead us to think that our emotions are somehow wrong or faulty in some way. I don't believe that they are. Studies show that 80% of daily thoughts tend to have a negative element to them. Humans are naturally a little negative by nature. At times everyone feels insecure, vulnerable, anxious, miserable and not good enough; this is just part of being a normal human being. These are normal natural emotions. They are not wrong.

On top of that you have bulimia, it is destroying your life, it is making you miserable and slowly killing you. How can you be expected to feel happy, confident and secure? Your emotions and feelings are not faulty. You are normal. Putting the blame on negative emotions only makes you feel worse whenever you do experience a negative emotion (which is inevitable). It's like adding misery on top of misery.

**Does an Emotional Binge Urge mean my brain is faulty?**

Many bulimics wrongly believe that having an urge to binge on food means they are broken and messed up. This mistaken association can make you feel more miserable, stressed and anxious every time you experience a binge urge.

Your brain is not faulty because you experience urges to binge on food. This is not a reflection on you as a person. As long as you are feeding your body the nutrition it needs (structured eating will help here!), your Emotional binge urge means nothing. It's simply an automatic habitual reaction, it's not a personal inadequacy. Your brain has been conditioned to crave a binge under certain conditions, that's all.

# The binge urge is just a feeling, it cannot control you

The urge to binge on food isn't going to disappear over night. Chances are you will experience urges to binge on food for at least a few months into your recovery. These binge urges are inevitable. You won't have any control over when they arrive, how strong they will be or how long they will stay. They seem to have a life of their own and you have no choice but to go along for the ride. This is not a failing on your part. This is just the nature of the urge itself.

When you experience strong feelings, there is a tendency to respond as though you are powerless against the feelings. The truth is, even at its strongest, the binge urge is just one aspect of your experience. As such, it is something separate from the "You" that is experiencing it. You are not your binge urge any more than you are this book. The binge urge, this book, and the words you are reading are all parts of your experience. As the experiencer, you are "bigger" than your experience. The binge urge is just a feeling and an experience, like any other feeling or experience. It doesn't have the power to control you.

For example, should you find yourself going towards the fridge for a binge, the very moment you notice your body reacting with movement... stop moving. Stand completely still. Realize that your thoughts cannot make you move. Realize your body is totally unaffected. The urge to binge is powerless unless you act on it. You may feel waves or a compulsion to binge, but they cannot make you move.

................................................................................

As author of Brain over Binge, Kathryn Hansen states:
*"The urge to binge comes from an older part of the brain in terms of evolutionary history - the primitive brain or lower brain. The lower brain generates our instinctual drives for food, water, oxygen, and other things it senses are necessary for survival. This is the part of the brain that produces "primal hunger" - the adaptive response to dieting - which leads to binge eating.*

................................................................................

The good news is that you are more than your lower brain. Your true self, residing in the higher-functioning, rational part of your uniquely human brain, has the capacity to override the automatic, primitive urges from your lower brain. No matter what thoughts, feelings, or cravings your lower brain generates, you always remain in control of your actions."

In recovery it can be helpful to keep in mind that although we cannot control our binge urges this does not mean that we are powerless against them.

## An attitude of acceptance

For many bulimics in recovery, whenever they first notice an urge to binge on food, their reaction is usually fear, panic and a deep desire to get rid of the urge as fast as possible. They may fight and argue against the binge urge in an attempt to throttle it out of existence. Unfortunately trying to wrangle or eliminate the binge urge often worsens it. We become frustrated that our attempts to control the urge are not working. We panic because the urge is not going away or because it is becoming more intense. We judge ourselves harshly and we begin to feel more crazed and out of control.

In reality we have very little control over how the urge to binge makes us feel, how long it stays, or how intense it is. We could try to argue against the binge urge with logic and reasoning but this isn't very effective. The emotional urge to binge comes from the lower brain and it's too primitive to understand rational arguments. You could have the most compelling arguments in the world not to binge, but it still isn't going to get rid of the urge to binge. It doesn't respond to logic, it operates at a subconscious level. Any attempts to control it are usually futile and perpetuate the idea that the binge urge is intolerable and that there is something wrong with you.

If you think about it. You don't binge because of your emotions or feelings. The only reason you binge is to remove your uncomfortable "urges to binge". If you could learn to be more accepting of your binge urges they wouldn't cause you as much bother and then you would be in a better position to ignore them rather than act on them.

**The psychology works likes this…**

106

Binge urge + panic and fear for having a binge urge = more uncomfortable emotions + stronger binge urges.

Alternatively,

Binge urge + acceptance that it's okay to feel this way for now = less uncomfortable emotions + less intense binge urges.

An attitude of acceptance can work wonders to diffuse the intensity of the binge urge. Acceptance is the art of learning how to be comfortable with feeling uncomfortable. Acceptance is a skill and like all skills it can be learnt and strengthened through continual practice.

# Accept, Delay and Distract

The Accept, Delay and Distract technique is a 4 step process you can apply when the binge urge strikes. Many of the people whom we coach, regularly use this exercise to successfully avoid bingeing.

With practice, this technique will help to weaken the binge urge conditioning and in time the binge urges will gradually fade away. This technique will also help you to see the truth about your urges—that they are meaningless, impersonal and fleeting.

I must stress this technique will only work if you are also feeding your body the appropriate amount of calories and nutrition it needs. If your binge urge is due to physical hunger then you need to eat more calorie-dense, nutrient-rich food in your meals or your binge urges will never go away.

## The Accept, Delay and Distract technique (The A.D.D technique):

### Step 1. Accept the binge urge

Although we have no control over our binge urges, we do have full control over how we react to them. Instead of fruitlessly attempting to control the binge urge, it is more effective to accept its presence and let the urge flow through you and do as it pleases. Remind yourself that the binge urge is just a feeling, it is not dangerous and does not need to be fought. Allow the urge to rise and fall again. Acceptance feels like a softening, a feeling that it's okay to be like this.

Two statements that you might want to say to yourself to reinforce your acceptance are: "It's okay to be uncomfortable right now." and "I can handle these feelings."

No matter how strong the feelings are, remind yourself that you do not want to binge. The real you does not want to binge. Allow the feelings to be, but keep resisting what the feelings are telling you to do. You can just tell the binge urge "I don't have to listen to you".

Try not to think of the binge urge as meaningful or compelling. Don't give it any more weight than it deserves. As long as you have stopped restricting and are providing your body food regularly then you can be certain that the binge urge means nothing.

See that you're okay. There is nothing to fear. These feelings and sensations cannot harm or hurt you. It is OK to feel this way. We tend to want to act on our urges right away or we panic. I'm not sure what we think will happen if we don't act on the urge, but it becomes very urgent. Instead, sit and watch the urge and realize that you're OK even if you don't act on it. The world doesn't end.

I am not asking to like the binge urge. I am sure you would rather the feeling wasn't there. That's understandable. But you don't have to struggle and fight it, that would just be adding suffering to suffering. The bottom line is that the feeling of a binge urge is less than ideal, but it is not intolerable.

There is no need to judge yourself harshly or feel guilty or ashamed for experiencing a binge urge. The emotional binge urge has nothing to do with you, your upbringing, your emotions or your self-esteem. It is not a reflection on who you are as a person. It's just the unthinking part of the brain that reacts automatically because of instincts and habit. Just think of it as brain junk. You can dismiss it. This isn't the real you.

## Step 2: Delay bingeing for 10 minutes

When you tell yourself that you have to make it through the rest of the night (or the rest of your life) without bingeing, the emotional burden of that commitment can become overwhelming, so instead, challenge yourself to resist bingeing for just 10 minutes at a time. This way you are far more likely to succeed.

As much as the binge urge may try to consume you, try to accept any sensations with a sense of calm. Tell yourself that if you still want to binge after ten minutes has passed then that's okay. Use a watch, or your phone to make a note of the time and try to wait a full 10 minutes before making any decisions as to whether or not you will binge.

## Step 3: Distract yourself

A binge urge does a great job of claiming your attention and your focus. Psychologists know that concentrating on two things at the same time is very hard. Therefore, if your mind is flooded with binge thoughts, do something else to distract yourself. Don't just stare at the clock waiting for 10 minutes to pass. Allow the urge to come and go as it pleases, stop struggling and move your attention and focus on something else.

If you are looking for ideas for something to distract yourself I would suggest something that involves physical movement and also takes you away from any possible binge foods. Something as simple as going for a walk can be extremely effective.

Here are some other suggestions:
- Go for a short jog.
- Go for a drive.
- Have a bath.
- Surf the web.
- Talk to a friend.
- Work or play on your computer.
- Immerse yourself in a project or hobby.
- Listen to your favorite music.
- Work in the garden.
- If you have children, play some games with them.

Distraction exercises may not take your mind off bingeing completely, but they should lesson the intensity of those urges. Remain interested in what you are doing and just let the binge urge be. Try not to get emotionally involved with the binge urge and accept it's existence. Remind yourself that "It's okay to be uncomfortable right now" and "I can handle these feelings."

## Step 4: Delay for a further 10 minutes if possible

Then, when the ten minutes is up, congratulate yourself for resisting the binge urge for a full 10 minutes. Well done! Even small steps like this can go a long way to weakening your urges.

After 10 minutes you may find the urge to binge is still quite strong. Challenge yourself to accept these sensations and feelings for another 10 minutes. Remind yourself that the binge urge is just a feeling. It cannot harm you. It cannot control you. You are more than your urge to binge. Encourage an attitude of acceptance to any sensations and feelings.

Alternatively, if after 10 minutes you are no longer able to resist the urge any longer then give yourself permission to binge. But remember that you are in control and it was your choice to binge.

If you continue to resist long enough eventually the binge urge will pass. It might take 5 minutes, 20 minutes or longer, but it will pass.

Repeat this process as many times as the urge arises. As you continue to practice this technique you will notice the length of time you are able to resist a binge urge increasing. Your binge urges will become less intense and frequent, until they eventually disappear altogether.

....................................................................................................

*"For a lot of time in recovery I used this technique, especially when trying to break free from a cycle of relapse and it really did work wonders. It is one of the most simple but powerful strategies you can use for overcoming relapse." - Sensa*

....................................................................................................

## This takes practice

Putting a stop to binging and purging takes time and practice, so it's quite normal to find yourself continuing to binge on food, especially in the first few months of your recovery. Please do not beat yourself up if you do end up binging. Remember that you are not expected to just stop bingeing in recovery. Don't put too much pressure on yourself to "never binge again".

We are all human, no one is perfect, so don't expect yourself to be any different. If you do binge, the most important thing to do is to resist the urge to purge and to get back onto your structured eating plan as soon as possible.

....................................................................................................

*"I remember my 3rd week into recovery my husband had to leave for a two week business trip. Up to this point I was doing great in recovery but a few days into his trip, my two small children had put me over the edge. They were fighting, crying and sick and so badly I just wanted to take myself to the store and buy as many candy bars as I could see. Instead, I fought back. I took my phone and texted my spouse telling him the immense amount of stress I was feeling. He quickly texted*

*back that I must distract or change what I was currently doing. I ran downstairs and began playing with my children, jumping around and singing with my kids, and within 20 minutes the urge was gone. At that moment I realized I was in control. It didn't need to control me." - Laura J*

## FAQ's

### I find it difficult to accept any binge urges, what should I do?

Accepting a binge urge can be challenging. If you find it difficult I recommend you play around with this and try different strategies to see what works best for you. You might find it helpful to imagine your binge urge as coming from a non-threatening cartoon character such as Buzz Lightyear or Mickey Mouse.

"I imagine myself like in a police shoot (really silly I know) and say to myself STOP! put your hands up and walk away from the binge." - Nora

"One thing I did was to expect the cravings to be worse than I knew they would be. This might just stress people out, but it worked for me. I would briefly think of more intense forms of pain and then think, "All this is, is pain. And, it's not the worst pain of my life. This is doable." - Jennifer

### My mind won't stop panicking, what should I do?

The binge urge can make you anxious and when you are anxious, your brain starts coming up with all sorts of outlandish thoughts.

You may have thoughts such as:
- "This urge to binge is going to kill me".
- "What's wrong with me? I'm going crazy!".
- "I am never going to recover I might as well binge".
- "My urges are not going away.... they are getting stronger". "This isn't working".
- "I will always have bulimia, I am a stupid for thinking I could ever get better".

These types of anxious thoughts are very common and unfortunately only serve to heighten your already anxious state. Again I recommend you apply an attitude of acceptance to these thoughts.

Studies show that we don't have any control over our thoughts. Our thoughts seem to have a life of their own. Just observe that you are having these thoughts and understand that it's all part of the process. Realize that we all have silly, uncontrollable, crazy thoughts all the time and this is normal. You are not weird for having weird thoughts.

Also, understand that your thoughts may be a little more negative right now as you are likely suffering the side effects of malnutrition and having to deal with the fear and uncertainty of starting recovery. In time, as you get used to recovery and as your body's delicate chemistry rebalances your well-being, your thoughts and feelings will improve and become more positive. For now just accept these thoughts, try to ignore them and let them be.

......................................................................................................

*"I remember the first time I sat through a negative binge/purge urge. This was sooo tough. After the urge passed I felt on top of the world because I had conquered the urge. I did not die because I was so uncomfortable" - Jessie*

......................................................................................................

# Bringing Awareness To a Binge

If you do find yourself bingeing on food, try out this simple technique to bring awareness to a binge.

For many of us, when we start bingeing our brain just shuts down, we go into a daze and we don't even think about what we are doing. Some call this the "binge trance".

However it can be helpful to shake ourselves out of this trance and bring some awareness to what we are doing. We may find that when we pay attention to what we are eating that we become satisfied much sooner which can lead us to eating less food and having smaller binges. We may also find that binges do not give us the same level of satisfaction as before and this will make letting go of bingeing easier.

The trick is to try to be more aware of what you are doing whilst you do it. As soon as you realize you are bingeing (or about to binge) start to pay attention to everything that you are doing in those moments.

Talk to yourself. Say out loud exactly what you are doing (or clearly in your mind if others are around you). If you are grabbing some biscuits say out loud, "I am grabbing some biscuits". Pay attention. As you eat the biscuits start paying attention to your jaw, the taste of each bite, the texture. When the second biscuit goes in, do the same. Does the second taste the same as the first?

Try to avoid going into the binge trance and keep the awareness going. Our taste response lowers when we are full, draw awareness to this, notice how things that normally taste really sweet lose that sweetness they had at the beginning. Everything starts to taste the same.

Remember, at any moment you can stop the binge-purge cycle, even when you think you've already taken action towards a binge. You may find that by paying attention you are able to stop your binge a lot sooner than usual. Give it a go over the next week or so and see if it helps.

# Pre-Emptive Binge Strategies

Stress and exhaustion can make you emotionally sensitive and prone to volatile, uncomfortable triggering emotions. In the middle of a full blown binge urge it can be challenging to manage your overwhelming emotions, so instead it's best to focus on lowering your stress levels in the days and weeks beforehand. You can think of this as 'pre-emptive' relaxation. You can do this by giving your mind, body and your emotions some much needed time to rest and recuperate.

Here are some strategies you can apply:

### Pre-Emptive Strategy 1: Schedule a Daily Time Out Session.

It can be helpful to schedule a daily Time Out Session for relaxation. Aim to set aside at least 20 minutes daily for your Time Out Session, but you can go longer if you choose. Try to make it a regular time such as before bed, in the morning or after a meal. Make this part of your daily routine and make it convenient so that you do it daily. Perhaps schedule this into your calendar to make it more official and less likely that you will skip it.

During the Time Out Session give yourself full permission to set aside your worries, responsibilities, tasks to be done, future plans and past regrets. You can worry about these issues later, but for now during this Time Out Session you give yourself full permission to let go, relax and hangout in any way that you choose.

It's best to turn off all gadgets and devices (yes, that means no email, Facebook or Twitter) and find somewhere quiet and restful. This is your time to be you, within yourself.

During this time you can enjoy doing nothing at all and feel good about taking a few moments to just be. You are free to do whatever you please, you can take a nap, read a favorite book, do some meditation, journaling, breathing exercises, yoga. Do whatever you feel like doing that will also allow you to recharge your batteries and re-energize your soul.

Spending time with yourself can be a deeply rewarding experience that will allow you to be much more comfortable with who you really are. For many people this can be the first step towards developing a more nurturing, loving attitude towards themselves.

You can notice how it feels good to relax and take the pressure off. Notice the gentle softening of your mind and muscles. Notice yourself breathing a little slower and deeper. Notice how your mind feels calmer, more settled and more at peace.

For some, taking a Time Out might not be so easy. Initially you may feel a little uncomfortable and awkward, you might think this is silly, useless, a waste of time or that you don't deserve to relax. These type of thoughts usually stem from an underlying fear of being alone with yourself and your mind without distractions. Reconnecting with yourself can feel a little overwhelming and scary when you are not even sure who you are or if you will even like yourself when you meet that person. Go slowly and gently, start with a short time period and tentatively increase the length of time as you feel ready. In time you will realize that there was nothing to fear.

If you lead a very busy life or have lots of important responsibilities then you may feel that it is 'impossible' for you to take time out for yourself. You may experience feelings of guilt or obsessively think about all of the things you 'should' be doing when relaxing. However, a growing body of multidisciplinary research is showing that relaxation and down time actually works to boost productivity, focus, work performance, and boost health. So you'll actually get more done and be able to cope with your responsibilities more effectively when you get into the habit of giving yourself regular time out.

Also please keep in mind that you deserve time to relax. You do not need to be busy at every moment of your life. It is okay to relax. It is okay to be not busy.

If you feel guilty, then think of it this as the most generous thing you can do for yourself and your friends and family. Once you recover your energy levels, your well-being will soar. Everyone in your life can benefit from a happier, healthier energized you, so please do not feel guilty about taking this time for yourself. The more you practice this, the easier it will become and the less guilt you will feel.

As with any discipline, the hardest part of making this change will be establishing it as a new habit, but regular practice will help. The more you can get into the habit of relaxing, the more you will benefit from doing so. Try to practice some conscious relaxation time each day if you can.

**FREE BONUS:** To help you relax I have recorded a helpful 20 minute meditation audio track for you. This meditation track will help you to reprogram your old eating habits at a sub-conscious level, boost your self-image and help you feel more calm and grounded. Go to **www.bulimiahelp.org/bonus** to download your free meditation audio track.

## Pre-Emptive Strategy 2: Get a good nights sleep.

Bulimia is exhausting. Really exhausting. It drains all aspects of your wellbeing.

- You're physically exhausted due to bad eating habits and malnutrition.
- You're mentally exhausted due to habitual worry, stress and anxiety.
- You're emotionally exhausted due to the loneliness, isolation and general sadness caused by bulimia.

Exhaustion can lead to increased anxiety, stress, mood swings and obsessive behaviour. To combat this, you simply need to rest. The easiest place to start is with a good nights sleep.

A good nights sleep can do wonders for improving your general wellbeing and increasing your emotional stability. Not only that but a lack of sleep can have a detrimental effect on your eating habits. "When you have sleep deprivation and are running on low energy, you automatically go for a bag of potato chips or other comfort foods," says Susan Zafarlotfi, PhD, clinical director of the Institute for Sleep and Wake Disorders at Hackensack University Medical Center in New Jersey.

The two hormones that are key in this process are ghrelin and leptin. "Ghrelin is the 'go' hormone that tells you when to eat, and when you are sleep-deprived, you have more ghrelin," explains Michael Breus, PhD, author of Beauty Sleep and the clinical director of the sleep division for Arrowhead Health in Glendale, Arizona. He also states that "Leptin is the hormone that tells you to stop eating, and when you are sleep deprived, you have less leptin. You are eating more, plus your metabolism is slower when you are sleep-deprived,"

Not only does sleep loss appear to stimulate appetite, it also stimulates cravings for high-fat, high-carbohydrate foods. This is not helpful if we are trying to recover from an eating disorder.

Experts recommend you get 7-8 hours sleep each night. If you can't make 7-8 hours, try to nap to make up for lost sleep. The best time for a nap is between 12pm and 3pm, at which point your melatonin levels are highest and your energy level tends to be lowest. Grabbing 10-20 minutes of rest is usually best for a middle-of-the-day nap. It can be helpful to set an alarm, even if it's only 15 minutes from now, to wake you back up and get you back to whatever you've got to do.

..............................................................................................................

*"I absolutely needed at least 7 hours sleep a night. It made such a huge difference and if I didn't get my sleep I was prone to binge urges the next day." - Pollyanna M.*

..............................................................................................................

## Pre-Emptive Strategy 3: Journaling

Many researchers now seem to be in agreement that regular journalling helps to reduce anxiety, improve mood, reduce stress and increase our overall levels of life satisfaction, while some studies even go on to show that keeping a journal can significantly boost your immune system, reduce your blood pressure, and improve your memory (Baikie and Wilhelm, 2005). Findings suggest that the lasting positive effects produced are similar to the positive effects produced by other psychological therapies and interventions. (Smyth, 1998) (Frisina, et al. 2004).

Journaling can help provide a safe space for you to begin being more honest with yourself about your thoughts and feelings in recovery. It will help you to stop "burying your head in the sand", or allowing yourself to make choices that deep down you know are harming your recovery.

### Tips for starting your very own journal...

There is no clear consensus regarding the best techniques for journaling but using something called 'stream of consciousness journaling' is a great place to start. Simply sit down for an allotted amount of time [15 minutes if you can] and write whatever comes to mind. Begin the first sentence with whatever comes to your mind, whether it's important, silly, random, whatever it is, just let it flow. Let the words flow. Allow yourself to release the pain you're feeling inside. Don't worry about the sentence structure or using the correct grammar or punctuation marks. They are not important. The important thing is that in this time you allow your soul to talk and that you give yourself the emotional release you're craving.

Think of this exercise as a cleanser for the mind, it's a way to "mentally purge" negative thoughts before they have a chance to build up and overwhelm you. Writing about your feelings can be a great method for alleviating mental anxiety, obsessive thoughts and releasing emotional stress.

You may choose to read what you've written at the end, or simply leave it and move on with your day, but hopefully you will notice yourself feeling a little less overwhelmed by your emotions.

Journaling is a good way to keep your hands and mind busy so as to not binge. Usually the evening is usually the best time for journaling as it is the most challenging time, but some people like to write in the morning.

Results from journaling research showed that sometimes people feel a temporary increase in anxiety or feel upset when they first start to write in this way, so give yourself time to adjust before deciding whether journaling is a good recovery strategy for you. If you don't enjoy journaling then it is perfectly okay not to do it.

.......................................................................................................................

*"To me, my journal became one of the most important tools in my journey of self-healing. All the points above agree with my experience; the challenge in the beginning to overcome the rising anxiety, the fear of not writing correctly, the block to just let go, and the final HUGE release after I really got going. Just let it all out and don't worry about what you are writing. JUST WRITE." - Tia*

.......................................................................................................................

## Other Strategies

You may want to apply other stress reduction strategies to your life such as yoga, deep breathing, going for a walk, moderate exercise, or simply talking it out with someone. I could easily fill this book with stress reduction strategies, but relaxation is so subjective and personal that instead I wish to encourage you to explore and discover what works best for you. Follow your own lead for what works best for recharging your batteries.

Although emotional/stress management can go a long way to preventing an emotional binge urge. Please don't think of these strategies as being a hundred percent foolproof. Even when you work to reduce your stress levels you may still experience binge urges (but perhaps they won't be so intense or as frequent). If you do experience an emotional binge urge then use the Accept, Delay and Distract technique.

# Getting Rid of Triggers

Early in recovery if you know something is a trigger for you it does makes sense to try and avoid it. There is no need to put yourself under unnecessary pressure. However, while it can be helpful to avoid triggers in the short term, in the long term it's not an effective solution. The problem is that in reality everything and anything could be a trigger: a fleeting negative thought, a television advert, a family member, a Facebook post, feeling bored etc. This makes it nearly impossible to avoid all triggers. Ultimately, for lifelong recovery we don't want to get rid of all of our triggers, instead we want to learn how to feel more comfortable with them so they don't cause us so much bother.

In saying that, here are some strategies you may find helpful when starting out in recovery.

## Clear out your home
- Spend an hour and go through your house clearing out any potential triggers.
- Studies show we are more likely to eat the first foods that we see so keep binge foods hidden from view or better yet don't have them in your house at all.
- If you live with someone else and you can't get rid of or hide food ask them if they'd be willing to put triggering foods away, or cut down on how much they buy.
- Hide your scales or throw them out.
- Remove any skinny clothes that you aspire to fit into.
- Throw out any fashion magazines.
- Get rid of anything else that may be a trigger for you.

If you cannot throw anything out, try storing those things away where they will not be seen. Perhaps in your attic or in an outside shed. Hopefully you will find this to be a very liberating and freeing activity.


## Keep Yourself Busy
When starting out in recovery big empty gaps in the day when you are bored can easily lead to a binge episode. Keeping yourself busy can work really well as a distraction.

How to keep yourself busy:

- Buy yourself a daily planner so you can stay organized.
- Break your day into 1 hour chunks and make sure you have something happening during each hour.

..................................................................................................

*"This is so useful. I remember when whole days used to just disappear in binge purge cycles when I was working from home on my thesis. Making a plan for each part of the day so that your time is not idle can be really useful even if it's just as simple as 8am go for a walk, 9am catch up on email, 10am, coffee, read paper etc..." - Alicia E*

..................................................................................................

# Strategies to Stop Purging

You are not expected to just stop bingeing but if you do binge do try to resist purging.

Vomiting after eating is the most common form of purging for people with bulimia. However, there are also other forms of purging such as abusing laxatives, over-exercising, taking diet pills, misusing diuretics and fasting for extended periods of time.

Some people use only one means of getting rid of food while others use a combination of methods. The ultimate goal of these methods is to rid the body of calories consumed and prevent weight gain. Unfortunately, these habits are neither effective nor healthy and can wreak havoc on your body, causing long-term health complications and even death.

Purging doesn't help to control your weight and in fact studies have shown that bingeing and purging can lead to weight gain (Agras and Apple, 1997). The problem is that all methods of purging are highly ineffective at removing calories from the body. Research shows that people who binged and then vomited still retained 1,000 to 1,200 calories after vomiting. So with any type of bingeing and purging, chances are you are consuming more calories than if you didn't binge and you just ate normal portions of food throughout the day.

Even if you feel 'empty' after vomiting, you are probably dehydrated, which can lead to more binge urges and salt cravings. Also, as your body responds to the food you have eaten, it releases insulin. When you throw up the contents of your stomach, it leaves too much insulin in your body. This leads to more sugar cravings!

Although your recovery should not be fear-based, you may find more motivation in knowing what the dangers are. According to the US National Library of Medicine, the following can result from purging:

- Hair loss and brittle fingernails.
- Teeth cavities or gum infections.
- Broken blood vessels in the eyes.
- Irritated or infected sinuses.
- Skin rashes and acne.
- Swollen or infected glands.

- Overall swollen appearance of the face, particularly the cheeks.
- Irritation or damage to the lining of the stomach and esophagus.
- Hypokalemia (low potassium) which can result in abnormal heart rhythms, fatigue, constipation and muscular damage.
- Amenorrhea (irregular periods).
- Edema (swelling) of the body due to water retention and dehydration.
- Russell's Sign - visible scars and calluses on the hands.

If you are feeling anxious and wish to purge, remind yourself that purging is not effective for weight management. By truly believing this, you are helping to remove the anxiety and fear of having food in your stomach. It is this anxiety and fear that leads to purging in the first place. Your body can handle the food. In fact, your body will actually thank you for feeding it by firing up your metabolism and reducing your binge urges.

Let's look at some strategies to help you stop purging:

## Strategies to Stop Purging 1: Accept, Delay and Distract

The Accept, Distract and Delay technique can be useful to help prevent you from purging.

### Step 1. Accept the urge to purge

Acceptance is your initial position, your opening stance. To begin with accept that you are experiencing an urge to purge. Perhaps your stomach feels uncomfortably full or perhaps you wish to purge your food as a release from anxious, stressful feelings. Try to accept those feelings in the present moment. You don't have to like the feelings, just accept that they are here right now and that there isn't much you can do about them. Know that in time these uncomfortable feelings will pass. There is nothing to fear, these feelings cannot harm you. If you are able to accept these sensations you will notice that they will sit with you much more comfortably.

### Step 2. Delay purging for 10 minutes

When you feel the urge to purge, try to delay taking any action towards it for at least ten minutes. As much as the urge may try to consume you, try to calm and reassure yourself by looking at the clock and waiting it out. Tell yourself that if you still want to purge after ten minutes has passed then that's okay - but first, you're going to wait it out.

### Step 3. Distract yourself

Try to distract yourself within the 10 minutes. Go for a short walk, phone a friend, do some yoga. Also throughout this time keep an attitude of acceptance going. If your stomach still feels uncomfortable try to embrace and accept that feeling. Remind yourself that there is nothing to fear. Food in your stomach will not turn to fat. Food in your stomach will help to heal you and reduce your binge urges.

### Step 4. Delay for a further 10 minutes if possible

Then, when the ten minutes is up, even if you still find the urge to purge is quite strong, see if you can go another ten minutes. Over the next few weeks try to increase the length of time you manage to go without purging.

## Strategies to Stop Purging 2: Create a new routine for after meals

Purging after a meal can become a habit. We need to break that habit. One effective technique to do this is to create a brand new routine to follow meal times. As soon as your meal is finished, do something different, something you don't normally do. Try a new hobby, go for a walk, play with the dog, phone someone, do a crossword, do anything that is different from your usual routine. Just make sure that there is no reason for you to visit the bathroom for at least 30 minutes after your meal because sometimes just seeing the toilet can act as a powerful purge trigger.

Stick to your new routine until it becomes a habit (this usually takes around 30 days). Once it becomes a habit you will begin to associate the end of a meal with your new routine, rather than it being time to purge. It's understandable that you may not be able to follow this routine exactly every time you eat, but try to stick to it when you can, it should have a really positive impact on your recovery.

## Strategies to Stop Purging 3: Cutting Back on Laxatives

For weight loss, very few things are as ineffective as laxatives. Laxatives do not help you lose weight, they only help you visit the toilet. Absorption of calories occurs high in the digestive system, whilst laxatives and diuretics influence the lower area.

After taking laxatives it may appear that you've lost weight, but any weight loss you do notice is due to water loss and dehydration only. It will rapidly return once you become rehydrated.

Take your time reducing your laxative intake. Don't stop cold turkey. You need to give your digestive system time to adjust so please consult your doctor before trying any laxatives reduction strategies.

**Prepare a laxative reduction strategy using the following steps:**
1. Make a note of the amount of laxatives you usually take throughout the week.
2. Set yourself a realistic reduction goal, for example if you currently take 4 laxatives each day then perhaps you can challenge yourself to cut this down to 2 each day. If that's too much, then consider cutting down on the amount you take every other day to start with.
3. Once you are comfortable with this, reduce the amount you are taking even further until eventually you have stopped altogether.


## Strategies to Stop Purging 4: Cutting back on Excessive Exercise

A sure sign of a developing exercise compulsion is pushing your body to exercise even when you feel too tired or drained to do so. Of course we all need a little push to motivate ourselves to exercise some times, but this is more than that, this is a relentless drive to exercise no matter what your body is telling you.

Moderate exercise is great for dealing with emotions in recovery, boosting endorphins and keeping healthy in general, but it is important to develop an awareness of where to draw the line. It is recommended that healthy adults engage in 20 minutes of low-to-moderate intensity exercise every day. If you enjoy more active exercise, it is recommended that you engage in 1 hour of more vigorous exercise 3-4 days a week.

Medical professionals advise that severely underweight people do not exercise at all and even keep all physical movements to a minimum.

**How to cut back on excessive exercising:**
1. Start by reducing the duration and or intensity of your workouts by a set amount each week. So either do shorter workouts or make them less intense
2. Over the next few weeks, decide which days will be your resting days where you do not perform any strenuous exercise. Commit to at least two days a week of rest. It is still okay to walk or do some gentle stretching, but keep the vigorous exercise to a minimum on these days.
3. Over time increase your number of rest days to three or even four. Keep in mind cutting back is the best thing you can do for your health, happiness and recovery.

If you like to stay fit you could search on google: "High Intensity Training (HIT)". You can achieve significant and measurable changes to your fitness by doing just three minutes of exercise a week according to new research, says Dr Michael Mosley.

### Do I have to stop working out entirely to recover?
No. A full recovery from bulimia means having a healthy relationship with food and your body. Exercise can be an important part of this relationship. In fact, moderate exercise can actually help to promote a healthy body image. The key is to break the addiction cycle of over-exercising, just as the binging and purging cycle must be broken.

...............................................................................................................

*"While exercise can be a great way to unwind, be honest with yourself as to what is a reasonable amount. Be careful that you don't overdo it. I had to set a limit on exercise or it would become another addiction for me like bulimia. 3-4 times a week maximum. I time myself. I cannot stay at the gym for more than an hour, from start to finish. When the end of the hour comes, I say no matter what, you are done. On the other days, I just find a way to be active: Taking walks, playing with my kids. Just important not to obsess." - Indy*

...............................................................................................................

# Dealing with Relapses

Everything in recovery can be going great for a few weeks or even months and then all of a sudden a binge/purge episode strikes out of the blue. Oh no, you have just relapsed!

This can be very upsetting and can really knock your confidence in recovery. You may think:

- You are a failure.
- That you are back to square one.
- That recovery is impossible.
- That recovery only happens for other people.
- That lifelong recovery never really happens for anyone.

These thoughts all boil down to one thing... Fear. A deep fear that you were fooling yourself all along and that you don't have what it takes to recover. A fear that you are doomed to live a life of bulimia.

I can tell you right now that these fears are nonsense. From the diversity of people and recoveries I have witnessed over the past few years, I can tell you without a doubt that no one is beyond help and that there is no such thing as being too weak or too broken for recovery. We have helped thousands of people overcome bulimia and nearly all of them relapsed multiple times and nearly all of them experienced those same fears. They felt devastated, gutted and disheartened, but they didn't give up on recovery and they made it. They are all now fully recovered. For inspiration you can view some of their success stories here: **www.bulimiahelp.org/success-stories.**

In truth, there is no such thing as a perfect recovery. You will experience a lot of ups and downs along the way. Including relapses. If you continue to binge for a few months whilst in recovery, that's okay, that's normal. In time, binge intensity and frequency will reduce. It's best to just think of relapses as a natural and normal part of the recovery process. Yes they are upsetting and I am sure you would prefer if they didn't happen, but nearly everyone experiences residual binge episodes when starting recovery. In time your conviction, faith and belief in recovery will grow, this in turn will help you to truly overcome the fear of relapses. When you realize you're never going to let bulimia win, there is no longer a need to fear relapsing.

*"I had this very powerful experience in recovery where I purged, but before I even left the bathroom I had this "conversation" with bulimia – I told my bulimia that it could make me relapse as much as it wanted, but that I was never going to give up. In that moment the fear just left, I knew relapsing couldn't destroy me." - Catherine Liberty, Recovery Coach*

## Treat yourself with compassion

An attitude of compassion can go a long way to healing any emotional pain caused by a relapse. Rest, take extra "you" time, talk to yourself kindly and remind yourself that this relapse was not your fault. Fully forgive yourself for the relapse and accept that it happened. Remember that there is no such thing as perfect recovery, you are making progress and that's what counts.

If you need to, go back to your structured eating plan as soon as possible, but feel free to choose foods that feel safer and easier for you to eat until you are feeling stronger.

Relapses can be exhausting and confusing experiences, but I really want to reassure you that whether you experience 5 relapses or 500 relapses throughout the course of your recovery, they're still not going to stop you from recovering unless you let them.

The trick is to make a commitment to learn from your relapses, to understand what they're trying to tell you, and to adjust your recovery accordingly. It's okay if you don't believe me right now, but I promise you that the insights you gain and the lessons you learn during episodes of relapse are what will make full recovery possible in the end.

## Analyzing a relapse

After a relapse, give yourself 5-10 minutes to figure out why it happened and how you can be better prepared in future.

### 1. Try to figure out why you relapsed

Put on your detective hat and ask yourself some of these questions to get more clarification about why you may have relapsed.

- Have you been restricting lately?
- Were you too hungry when you started eating?
- Were you paying attention as you ate?
- Did you pause or stop while eating?
- Did you eat too quickly?
- Did you have too much on your plate?
- Had you been depriving yourself of that particular food?
- Did you overeat because you feared you would deprive yourself of food later that day?
- Are you eating regular meals and snacks?
- Are you eating a variety of foods from all food groups? Or are you avoiding certain food groups e.g. fat?
- Are there gaps longer than 3 hours between your meals and snacks?
- Did you continue to eat because you didn't want the food to go to waste?
- Do you have a tendency to eat more at a certain time of the day?
- Did you binge to suppress other feelings?
- Are you feeling stressed?
- Did you try to Accept, Delay and Distract the binge urge?
- Are you encouraging an attitude of acceptance to any urges?
- Are you pushing yourself too hard in recovery?
- Were you too tired?
- Were you emotionally sensitive?
- Are you skipping meals?
- Are you purging after meals?
- Did you do an intense workout?
- Were you drinking alcohol or taking recreational drugs?
- Were there exceptional circumstances out of your control?
- Were you too far out of your normal comfort zone?

There may be lots of reasons, but if possible try to identify one main reason that caused you to relapse.

## 2. Ask yourself "what one step could I take in the future to try and prevent a relapse like this happening again?"

Figure out what you can do in future to help prevent the relapse happening again. For example, if you decided that it was an accumulation of stress that pushed you to the point of relapse that day, then it would make sense to focus on incorporating even more relaxation time into your days. Or perhaps looking for ways to make your days at work that little bit less stressful.

*"When my first relapse came I was beyond devastated. Some things I thought at the time of my initial relapse: My entire world is falling apart/ I knew recovery was impossible/ It was good while it lasted/ I am a failure/ I will never do this/ maybe after all it is impossible to recover from ten years of bulimia/ back to square one. In reality none of this was the truth. Thankfully something in me realized that and I stayed committed to recovery. I relapsed a few more times since then too but the thoughts that come along with relapsing really do change as recovery time goes by."*
*- Catherine Liberty*

# Common Challenges:
## "I'm really scared to do any of this!"

Recovery can be scary. Throughout many of the steps in this program (e.g. increasing your portion size, stopping purging, eating challenging foods) you will be confronting your fears head on. This can be challenging.

Fear is a powerful force that can hold people back from living their life to the full. For example some people never swim in the sea for fear of sharks or some people never travel by plane for fear of it crashing, although statistically the chances of those events happening are extremely slim. That's the problem with fear, it tends to override logical arguments.

As an example, you may tell yourself that eating a balanced meal is good for you and for your recovery, but you may still feel fearful when eating carbohydrates.

Or you may tell yourself that increasing your portion size will dramatically reduce your binge urge, but you may feel panicked when attempting to add more food to your plate.

So what should we do when we feel afraid?
Any time you feel a rush of fear or even a sense of panic following this program (e.g. your thoughts begin to race and your heart starts to pump faster), I want you to do one thing...

I want you to accept any sensations that you feel and let them be as they are.

This means, resist fighting any fear sensations, resist panicking because they exist, resist trying to get rid of them. If we fight fear it will only make it stronger.

Instead remind yourself that to really grow and evolve in recovery you need to push yourself out of your comfort zone and realize that yes, it can be scary, but really, try to accept this fear. It is okay to be afraid. Always remember, everyone feels afraid at times and this is okay.

Being afraid is just a sensation. It can not harm you, hurt you or control you. It's just a feeling within your body. Just like with binge urges, if you learn to accept and embrace any fear feelings they won't bother you so much and will not cause you as much discomfort. An attitude of acceptance is extremely powerful here.

If the anxious, fear feelings are very strong you may want to try this quick technique:

## Flow with Fear Technique

1. Find a comfortable place to sit down, close your eyes and relax for 10 minutes.
2. Tune into any fear sensations you are experiencing.
3. Try to feel the fear sensations rather than think about them.
4. Fall into the sensations. Melt into the feelings. Feel yourself wrapped in a cotton ball of sensation. Let it flow around you. Explore it. Feel it. Realize it cannot harm you in any way. Spend time with it. Realize you are safe.
5. Remind yourself that "It's okay to be uncomfortable right now" and "I can handle these feelings."
6. Let the feeling flow and change. In time you may feel it soften, or feel warmer or feel even comforting. Just let the sensation do what it needs to do and let it pass on its own accord.
7. After 10 minutes, or once you feel more comfortable, open your eyes and finish the session.
8. When you feel ready, at your own pace, face whatever it is that caused you fear in the first place. If you feel afraid again accept any sensations. It is okay to feel afraid. This is a positive sign that you are pushing forward in recovery.

This technique will help you to feel more comfortable with any fear sensations. In time and with practice you will realize that fears sensations are nothing to be afraid of. Once you are no longer afraid of 'feeling afraid', well then... nothing can stop you!

Also, remember to go slow in recovery, take baby steps if needed and then things won't seem so scary!

# Common Challenges:
## "What's with all this crying?"

Most bulimics learn to use their eating disorders as a way to mask and numb painful emotions, so it makes sense that when you start to live without bulimia for the very first time, your emotions are going to bubble up and vent out. It is very common to experience an increase in emotional mood swings at the start of your recovery. This is part of the process of change.

As your binge/ purge sessions become less frequent you may discover that some buried emotions start to be released. Sometimes you might feel depressed for no reason, sometimes your anxiety may increase even when everything is going well for you, and sometimes you're going to feel like hiding away from the world. The important thing to know is that this is not a sign of weakness, or a reflection on your ability to cope without your eating disorder in the long term. It is simply a natural, and temporary part of the healing process.

One of the most powerful steps you can take right now while you're experiencing erratic mood swings is to accept and embrace them as part of your recovery. I know you don't want to feel this way. I know that you may even feel embarrassed or 'crazy' when you're pushed to tears over the smallest of things, but what you need to realize is that you are going through some epically big changes right now. You are facing fears that have trapped you for years. You are turning your back on a life that only served to hurt you, and you are choosing recovery.

You don't have to over analyze these emotions, you don't have to make sense of them and you don't have to fear them. These emotions are not wrong or bad. They just are. You need to accept that this is part of the healing process. It's okay to feel hurt and it is okay to cry. Crying is good as it helps you to release stress hormones, so if you need to cry, then please have a cry. It can be healing in its own way.

Give yourself a big emotional hug and the next time you're experiencing a low mood try to offer yourself the same level of compassion and understanding as you would offer to a friend.

The good news is that most people find that any erratic mood swings and increases in anxiety tend to lessen within several months. Depression also tends to lessen naturally within the first 2-3 months of recovery. Afterwards you should see a great improvement in mood, emotional stability and general wellbeing.

........................................................................................................

*"This was the hardest thing for me in recovery, just as soon as I would start to become in control of my eating my emotions would spiral out of control and that would often scare me straight back into a relapse. I also found it hard because the emotions were so powerful and would appear so suddenly and I no longer knew why I was feeling them. In time I learnt to accept them and just let them be. This was a big moment for me." - Andrea*

........................................................................................................

# Common Challenges:
# "Help, I think I am developing Binge Eating Disorder!"

At the start of recovery some people do successfully stop bingeing and purging immediately. Most however, start by stopping purging and then they gradually reduce episodes of binge eating over time. When you stop purging it does take time for those binge urges to lessen. For some weeks or months you may find yourself bingeing but not purging, just like someone with a binge eating disorder would. This scares many people into believing that they are simply exchanging one eating disorder for another, but actually this is a very normal phase of recovery. No one expects you to immediately stop bingeing and purging forever at this stage. That would be unrealistic. In time your bingeing will become less frequent and will eventually stop altogether. Any weight gained through these binges will be temporary and will be lost naturally as you continue on with your recovery.

# Common Challenges:
# "What's the difference between overeating and bingeing?"

Overeating is a normal behavior everyone can experience from time to time. Perhaps your food tasted great. Perhaps you felt like clearing your plate. Perhaps you weren't really paying attention and accidentally ate a little too much. Whatever the reason, it is natural for people to overeat from time to time.

However, a binge is very different. Formal definitions of bingeing tend to say that it always involves eating "a large amount of food over a short period of time". While this is true for many people, in general a binge can be defined as 'loss of control' when eating, regardless of the quantity of food you've eaten.

**Other signs of bingeing are:**
- Eating to comfort unwanted thoughts and emotions.
- Entering a trance-like headspace.
- Eating very rapidly.
- Eating alone and experiencing feelings of shame, guilt, disgust and depression afterwards.

Overeating on the other hand has a number of subtle differences. So, after overeating you may still feel some guilt, but usually there are no feelings of loss of control. You have still eaten more food than your body needed at that time but the reasons are completely different. Accept that at times you may overeat. This is perfectly normal and should not cause unnecessary concern. It is unrealistic to expect eating to be perfect all the time.

# Tools: Measuring Progress in Recovery

People in recovery love to count the number of days since their last binge as an indication of their progress. Personally I do not recommend it. Counting days since your last binge can turn recovery into a waiting game. If a binge does happen it can feel like all your efforts have been a waste of time and you're back to square one.

A relapses does not actually mean you have failed and it does not mean that you are back to square one. The number of days since your last binge is not an accurate reflection of your progress in recovery (in fact it's only a small piece of the puzzle). If you must count the days since you relapsed, please remember that it is not a true indication of recovery or progress.

There are other more accurate signs of improvement that you can use to track your progress. After 1-3 months in recovery keep an eye out for some of these signs of progress (even if you are still bingeing).

## Signs of progress to look for include:
- Less frequent binges.
- Shorter binges.
- Binges on smaller amounts of food.
- The ability to stop/lose interest in the middle of a binge.
- Forgiving yourself more quickly after a binge ends.
- Bouncing back more quickly when a binge happens.
- Stopping a binge from happening even when the urge is present.
- Binge eating, but not purging.
- Feeling awake and energized each morning.
- Noticing decreased stress levels around food.
- An increased stability of your moods.
- An increased sense of wellbeing and inner peace.
- The ability to successfully cope with trigger environments.
- Spending less time obsessing or thinking about food.

Keep an eye out for these signs of progress in recovery as they will help to keep you motivated and encouraged.

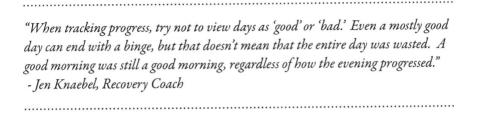

*"When tracking progress, try not to view days as 'good' or 'bad.' Even a mostly good day can end with a binge, but that doesn't mean that the entire day was wasted. A good morning was still a good morning, regardless of how the evening progressed."*
*- Jen Knaebel, Recovery Coach*

## Duration, Intensity and Frequency (DIF)

If you prefer to a have a more official indication of your progress you can try using D.I.F to map progress. This is a measure of the Duration, Intensity and Frequency of a binge out a scale of 1 to 10.

- **Duration:** How long did the binge last, from 1 to 10 (10 being very long)
- **Intensity:** How intense was the binge, from 1 to 10 (10 being very intense)
- **Frequency:** How long was the time between binges, from 1 to 10 (10 being very little time at all).

Each time you binge, score the duration, intensity and frequency. Then add up the three results to form your D.I.F score. At the end of each week add up your total D.I.F score for the week. The lower the score the better.

Keep in mind that recovery is not a linear process. Some weeks will be better than others. Don't get upset if you are successful one day, but fail the next. Measuring your weekly D.I.F score will help you keep an eye on the bigger picture. Please try not to measure success on a day-to-day basis as it's not very accurate. If you are no longer bingeing on food you can still measure the D.I.F score of your binge urges. You can then use this score as a marker for your progress.

# Stopping Bingeing and Purging:
## Super Short Version

As a helpful reminder, here is the super short version of "Stop Binging and Purging".

It's ok if you binge. You are not expected to just stop bingeing but if you do binge try to resist purging.

Your brain may have been conditioned at a subconscious level to have stronger cravings for food under certain emotional conditions. This is simply an automatic habitual reaction and it has nothing to do with your personality, upbringing or self-esteem. We can remove these binge urges by applying the Accept, Distract and Delay technique.

**The steps are:**
1. Accept the binge urge. Remind yourself that the binge urge is just a feeling, it cannot control you, it is not dangerous and does not need to be fought. Accept you have no real control over the binge urge and allow the urge to rise and fall again.
2. Delay taking any action towards your urge for the next 10 minutes.
3. Distract yourself during those 10 minutes.
4. If possible delay for another 10 minutes. Over the next few weeks try to increase the length of time you managed to go without bingeing.

(This technique can also be used to prevent purging).

If you do binge, try to avoid going into the binge trance by eating with full awareness of what you are doing when you are doing it. This can help to reduce the intensity and duration of the binge.

Other helpful strategies to reduce bingeing and purging include:
- Realize that purging is not effective for weight management.
- De-stress by taking a time out each day to relax and ensure you get a good nights sleep.
- Remove any potential triggers from your home environment.
- Keep busy throughout the day to help keep yourself distracted.
- Create a new routine for after meals to help prevent purging.
- Gradually cut back on excessive exercise and laxatives.

- Accept relapses as a natural part of recovery. After a relapse, give yourself 5-10 minutes to figure out why it happened and decide how you can be better prepared in future.

Don't forget you can go to **www.bulimiahelp.org/bonus** to download your free 20 minute meditation audio track. This meditation track will help you to reprogram your old eating habits at a sub-conscious level. It will boost your self image and help you to feel more calm and grounded.

# Cassie's Success Story

"For the past ten years and up until around 4 months ago, I was convinced that even if I really wanted to part with bulimia, I couldn't. I had tried and 'failed' so many times stooping lower with each defeat.

As a result I convinced myself that for all the harm I was doing to my body, my mind, my social life and my chances of being happy, the positives of my addiction outweighed the negatives. 'It's not that bad' I would tell myself. 'I can usually control myself', I would whisper to myself in those desperate moments when my secret came crashing down on my 'normal' life throwing it into disarray.

I was so certain that it gave me control and helped me cope as I sacrificed one aspect of my life after the other to be able to have the time to shop, binge, purge, hide and lie. I was too afraid to tell anyone what I was going through.

I had a friend who was tragically diagnosed with skin cancer. This was something that shook my world and put my obsession with my weight in perspective. We never know how long we have in this world nor can we decide. One thing I knew for sure: if I knew my time was limited, the last thing I would be thinking is 'I wish I had have been thinner in my life'.

I told my partner who was completely supportive. Telling him was the hardest thing I had ever done. I had to cry hysterically for 2 hours with him guessing what was wrong before I could even begin to talk!! But it was also the best thing I could have done.

Bulimia Help gave me the support I needed. I found people who seemed like amazing individuals and it made me realize I was not the problem – there are thousands of intelligent, beautiful men and women dealing with this problem and it is a tragedy that we blame ourselves!

One of the most important aspects of the Bulimia Help Method is that it made recovery seem plausible. It promised me that I could recover and gave me concrete steps that I would take to put me down that path. Most importantly, it made sense.

I didn't believe it at first. I followed the structured eating plan certain (and prepared) that I would gain weight. I felt like I was eating so much but was still getting hungry and 'slipping up'.

I really noticed a complete reduction in my urges to binge when I introduced previously 'forbidden' foods such as chocolates and sweets into my eating plan. It felt amazing the first few times I was able to eat chocolate without binging, have an ice cream or cake with friends. It took time, but it has transformed the role of food in my life from a fear to a pleasure

I have not put on any weight and after 2 months of eating pretty much what I feel like, when I feel like (still trying to be reasonably healthy but never restricting) I still can't believe how much my life has changed for the better.

I have rediscovered spontaneity! In the last few months I feel like I have gained hours of my day and the freedom to just relax and be a fully participating member of my life again!! I had forgotten what it felt like.

I feel like my life at the moment is more 'normal' than it has been at any point in my memory. It's strange; most days I think about how proud I am of how far I've come. Of how much better my life is. Nevertheless, there is still the shadow of my MIA. I still think about it. I have to remind myself of how horrible it was. I had been so wrong about everything that I thought MIA gave me. I want my life to be my own!"


~ Cassie

# Stage 3 in Recovery: Making Peace With Food

Congratulations you have reached stage 3 of recovery "Making Peace with food". I know we have already covered a lot of ground together and you are doing fantastic to still be with me. Please take a moment to pat yourself on the back. Seriously, please do. You deserve it, you are doing great!

You are a beautiful, wonderful, amazing person. Do you know why you are so amazing? Because you are a seeker. That's right. You seek out greatness in yourself. You know you were born to live your dreams and you are determined to not let bulimia hold you back any longer. Deep down I am hoping you are beginning to realize a truth... **you can do this, you are strong enough, you have what it takes, you can be free!**

Right now we are roughly halfway through the Bulimia Help Method. If you are reading through this book fully before starting your recovery (well done for being so pro-active!), I would recommend you focus on getting a handle on stages 1 & 2 first, before even starting stage 3. I know you are probably super keen to go through the program as fast as possible (I love your enthusiasm!), but stage 3 is where we begin to work on more advanced recovery strategies and if you haven't got a solid foundation in place, it won't be of much use to you. I would recommend you focus on stage 1 and 2 for AT LEAST a few weeks before starting stage 3. Our goal here is lifelong recovery, we need to be patient with ourselves and go through the program at a pace and speed that gives our body time to heal. For recovery it is better to be the tortoise rather than the hare.

In saying that, it's still a great idea to read through the rest of the book, as it will give you a deeper insight into how The Bulimia Help Method actually works and what the entire recovery process will entail.

## So let's gets started with stage 3... Let's make peace with food.

Years of living with bulimia can make you feel as though you are in an abusive relationship with food. Food terrifies you, undermines you, breaks you. You know you cannot live without food, yet you must eat. When you do eat food you experience surges of anxiety, fear and dread. You eat, freak out, binge and purge and desperately hope that tomorrow won't be as bad as today. This is not a good place to be.

Your war against food is based on a misunderstanding. You thought your binge urge was trying to harm you, hurt you and make you fat. In truth, your binge urge is a friend trying to protect you, heal you from your malnutrition and prevent you from feeling uncomfortable emotions. Whilst your binge urges had your best of intentions at heart, realize that they are no longer serving you. It's time to move on. Instead of fighting food we need to lay down our arms and make peace with food. The war is over.

In this stage, instead of fighting food you are going to make peace with food. You are going to learn how to:

- Let go of our food rules, so we can begin to release the power that food has over us. In time food will become just food.
- Listen to our hunger pangs throughout the day so that we can begin to learn what we are really craving and how to best satisfy that craving.
- Pay attention and eat slowly so we get a deeper understanding and knowledge of the relationship between our body and food.

..................................................................................

*"I realized my problem was not my body but my lack of understanding how to operate it. From that moment on, I stopped seeing it as the enemy that just wouldn't listen to me. I stopped trying to push it around and force it to do something against its will. Instead, I became its student, started listening to my body very closely and as a result, I started learning from my body." - Linda*

..................................................................................

# Making Peace With Food Step 1:
## Start to Eat "Sometimes" Foods

Food rules... "eat this... don't eat that... this is good... this is bad... only eat this before 7pm..."

We were not born with a list of foods that we should or shouldn't eat. We pick up food rules from magazines, TV, diet plans, diet gurus, parents, friends; anywhere and everywhere really. We want to eat healthy, we really do, so we try our best to follow these rules. Over time, as more rules get added to our list, the amount of acceptable foods we allow ourselves to eat shrinks. But our list of "safe foods" doesn't just get smaller and smaller, it also gets less satisfying and harder to stick to.

At the beginning our food rules were supposed to make us happier, healthier and more in control, but as time has gone on they have only made us more miserable and even more out of control. We mourn the loss of foods that we don't allow ourselves to eat and they have become extra special, tastier and more desirable. We miss the tasty flavors and joy of eating the banned foods, so we end up feeling miserable and deprived.

Eventually we become fed up, tired and frustrated with our rules and we eat something that isn't on our "safe foods" list. The moment of pleasure is quickly followed by guilt, shame, anxiety and fear. We may think "ah well, I have blown it now, I might as well go ahead and eat everything else on my bad foods list". This is a fast track to a full blown binge.

It isn't just bulimics who experience this. One study involving 2,075 adults found that 45% of them felt guilty after eating foods that they liked.

If you continue to avoid certain foods then you will always be vulnerable to being triggered by them. This is why reintroducing triggering foods, even the ones that you consider to be "un-healthy" or "bad" is such an important step to take in recovery. I am aware that some recovery methods advocate avoiding certain foods for life in order to recover, however I strongly disagree with this. It is just not true. In time you can learn to eat any type of food without feeling triggered. The first step to this is to begin to view food from a new, more realistic perspective.

## A new way to view food

In truth, there is no such thing as 'junk' food, 'rubbish' food or 'bad' food. These are just labels created by the latest so called expert or diet guru. Chocolate isn't necessarily "bad" and apples aren't inherently "good".

Instead, a healthier and more realistic way to view food is: "sometimes food" and "all the time food" because ideally you should eat certain foods more frequently than others. For example, eating foods like fruit and vegetables, meat/tofu, bread/rice/potatoes/pasta and oils each day, will promote good health, so we call these "all the time foods." While other, more "energy dense" foods like chocolate, ice-cream and chips should be eaten less frequently and can be thought of as "sometimes foods".

## Introducing "Sometimes Food" into your meal plan

To help you overcome food rules we are going to introduce a portion of "sometimes food" into your meal plan.

A "sometimes food" is food that you may have avoided in the past or a type of food that you might have only eaten when binge eating. A "sometimes food" may even be one of your favorite types of food or perhaps it's food that you tend to crave a lot of the time.

When adding a "sometimes food" into your meal plan it is highly recommended that you start slowly, take small steps and go at your own pace. Then over time, build up to including one or two portions of "sometimes food" into your meal plan every day. The goal here is to de-stigmatize the food so that it loses its power over you. Keeping that goal in mind, you can decide for yourself how often and when you will choose to eat your "sometimes food."

If you feel too much anxiety eating your "sometimes food" you may want to start with small portions first. Perhaps eat your "sometimes food" as a snack, or alternatively as a portion of a larger meal. If you are worried that eating a "sometimes food" could lead to a binge, try to buy small quantities of the food. That way even if you want to binge on it, you won't be able to. If this is not possible it is wise to throw away any leftovers immediately before you can be tempted to binge on them.

...........................................................................................................

*"Chocolate used to be one of my main trigger foods, so rather than eating it on it's own, initially I would have a little bit with oatmeal for breakfast. When it came to*

*eating pizza (another big trigger food of mine) I would have just one slice and then eat a salad with it, because I knew this would help me to get used to eating it without feeling very overwhelmed." - Catherine Liberty, Recovery Coach*

Giving yourself full permission to eat "sometimes food" may take a little getting used to. At first you may find that you want to eat these foods all of the time or that they awaken emotional binge urges. Don't worry, this is perfectly normal. In time, once you stop depriving yourself of these foods, your body will realize that there is nothing special about them.

You may feel that eating your "sometimes food" every day sounds like a lot. But keep in mind that eating "sometimes food" regularly can help to de-stigmatize the food, making it less desirable. It's not the food itself that leads to a binge; it's the anxiety and fear associated with eating the food. By avoiding specific foods completely you are only reaffirming this anxiety and fear. By confronting this fear, you will expose it as a fake and then these foods will quickly lose the anxiety and fear attached to them. Regular consumption of forbidden foods will prevent you from bingeing on them. You will no longer feel so deprived and miserable. You will start to find that prohibited foods lose their sparkle. Previously off limit foods that are tasted every day are said to not taste as good as previously imagined. Very soon, it will become evident that you can handle all foods and that they have no control over you and your recovery.

Try not to think of "sometimes food" as special treats to be eaten occasionally. They are not special treats. Do not make them more special than they really are. Sporadic consumption of the food is likely to make them more of a binge trigger.

## FAQs

### "But I want to eat only healthy foods. What should I do?"
Food recommendations that you may read in magazines, articles etc, are not meant to be taken to the extreme. "Eat more of this and less of that" does not mean "eat only this and none of that". People can easily read recommendations and warp them into what they think to be true.

We all know it's not healthy to live only on salads and vegetables. We also know it's not healthy to only eat low-fat foods all the time. It's also not healthy to completely avoid eating carbohydrates every day.

Lots of people determine the healthiness of food based on its calorie content alone, but doing so can mean you're missing out on essential nutrition, which in turn plays havoc with your health. Many so called "healthy" foods are so low in calories and nutrition that you'll find it almost impossible to satisfy your appetite, no matter how much you eat. You can fill your stomach with these foods but your body will still be crying out for more.

To be perfectly healthy you do not need to eat perfectly. It's recommended by health experts that you need a varied diet. You need to start to choose foods that you actually want to eat, rather than basing your food choices on how healthy you believe something is. Of course if you find yourself wanting to eat lots of very healthy foods like fruits and vegetables then that's okay too, but if you find that they are all you want to eat then you need to understand that while those foods have many health benefits, eating them alone is not healthy eating. You may want to assess if there are underlying motivations for those choices.

Ultimately, it's okay to want to eat healthily, as long as you truly understand what it means. The healthiness of your food intake is best assessed by looking at the overall picture. It is about balance, variety and developing a non-restrictive, non-judgmental eating attitude.

**"What are the dangers of just eating only very healthy foods during recovery?"**
You may or may not have heard about the lesser known eating disorder Orthorexia. It is an unhealthy obsession with health and "pure" food where a person restricts their eating to only specific "health" foods. It might not sound so bad, but extreme cases of Orthorexia have resulted in death.

..........................................................................................

*"I've struggled with both Bulimia and Orthorexia. My Orthorexia definitely stemmed from reading too many articles written by supposedly nutrition experts and health food blogs. Bottom line, any lifestyle that gives food ambiguous adjectives such as "good/ bad," "healthy/ dangerous" is ED prone. I think this is a major issue because there is a grave danger that many people trying to recover might trade their*

*bulimia for Orthorexia and consider themselves recovered, which could not be further from the truth." - Angel 42*

..................................................................................................................

..................................................................................................................

*"There is so much online about raw food diets etc...that have been really counter-productive to my recovery. I would think I was doing the right thing but really I was depriving my body in a whole different way." - BrightLove*

..................................................................................................................

### "But, I've been avoiding these foods for years, how can you expect me to just start eating them again?"

Although you may have been trying to avoid these foods, it's probably not stopped you from bingeing on them.

It's likely that you are going to eat these foods anyway, whether you try to avoid them or not. Would you rather have lots of candy all at once, or some small pieces of candy that you can enjoy over time without guilt? There is nothing to fear, trust that your body can handle it.

### "But I am scared to get rid of my food rules!"

The reason we fear letting go of our food rules is because we have been brainwashed into believing they are doing us justice. It takes time for this brainwashing to disappear. It is alright to be a little scared. Just take your time and introduce "sometimes foods" only when you are ready and safe. In time you will see that there is nothing to fear.

### "What if the trigger food causes a relapse?"

This does happen sometimes, but as you know by now, relapses are not a sign of failure. They are an opportunity for you to continue to learn and fine-tune your recovery. If you find that re-introducing trigger and challenge foods is causing you to continually relapse, then you can either go back to a small period of avoidance until you are feeling more confident, or you can keep going and focus on eating those foods in the safest way possible until urges to relapse disappear. If possible you should try to always opt for the latter choice.

### "When should I start this?"

The answer to this will be different for everyone. Some people prefer to eat "sometimes food" right from the start of recovery, while others like to have a period of avoidance before re-introducing them. Once you have a good structured eating foundation in place and you feel ready, make a start.

. . . . . . . . . . . . . . . . . . . . . . . . . . . . . . . . . . . . . . . . . . . . . . . . . . . . . . . . . . . . . . . . . . . . . . . . . . . . . . . . . . . . . . . .

*"For the first eight weeks of my recovery I avoided all of my trigger foods because I wanted to give myself the best start. It was hard enough learning to eat every 3 hours without having to worry about being triggered on top of that. After those eight weeks I gradually reintroduced most of my trigger foods. I tried to never buy them in large quantities and I tried to only eat them when I felt very safe and not too hungry. I think that really helped." - RunnerGirl*

. . . . . . . . . . . . . . . . . . . . . . . . . . . . . . . . . . . . . . . . . . . . . . . . . . . . . . . . . . . . . . . . . . . . . . . . . . . . . . . . . . . . . . . .

### "Can you provide a more detailed plan on how to do this?"

If you are having difficulty introducing "sometimes" food into your meal plan you can try to follow this helpful 4 step outline below:

### 1. Make a list of your favorite foods.

Make a list of your top 10 favorite foods. A lot of the time some of your favorite foods are only eaten as part of a binge. Acknowledge that these foods are important to you and by not eating them you will always feel deprived. This list may include foods that you have avoided since starting recovery and any additional foods that you consider to be "binge foods", "challenging foods", "bad foods" and "triggering foods". No foods are forbidden here.

### 2. Re-order your list starting with the safest food first.

It can be difficult to decide which of your trigger and challenge foods are the "safest" but usually there will be some foods that you feel would be far less challenging to start re-introducing. Ordering your list in this way will help you to start working on introducing the less challenging foods one at a time. It also means you won't need to start re-introducing the more difficult foods until you have progressed further in recovery.

### 3. Decide when and how you will re-introduce these foods

You've got your list of foods so now it's time to decide when and how you will start re-introducing them.

Start with the first food from your list and consider the following:

- How often will you include this food in your structured eating plan?
- Are there certain times of the day when you feel it would be easier to re-introduce this food?
- Are there certain situations when you may need to avoid eating this food?
- Will it be easier to re-introduce this food as a snack?
- Can you buy or prepare this food in small quantities so there will be no temptation to binge on left-overs?

### 4. Go for it!
You've decided which food you will reintroduce first, you've given a lot of thought to how and when you will do this, so now it's time to go for it. Work through your list reintroducing one food at a time.

### Summary
To help us overcome our harmful food rules, we can start adding portions of our favorite "sometimes foods" to our meal plan. Over time, build up to include one or two portions of "sometimes foods" to your meal plan everyday.

# Making Peace With Food Step 2:
# Mindful Eating

Bulimics tend to eat very quickly. When they do allow themselves to eat, they tend to stuff food down as fast as they possibly can. By eating food in a chaotic, tense and anxious way we associate eating food with chaos, tension and anxiety.

Instead, we want to associate eating food with feeling calm, nurtured and at peace. To do this we are going to start eating mindfully. This means eating more slowly and paying more attention during meal times.

A joint study conducted by Duke and Indiana State Universities revealed that binge eaters who participated in a nine-week program of mindful eating went from binge eating four times a week to just once a week.

Eating mindfully also helps to build the foundation for us to become "intuitive eaters" (stage 5) later on in recovery.

The two strategies we are going to use in order to become mindful eaters are:

## 1. Eating slowly

It's really helpful to get into the habit of eating slower during recovery. You don't have to eat at a snails pace, you just need to start eating your meals a little slower than usual. This will help you to accurately eat the right amount of food that is perfect for you. It takes about 20 - 30 minutes for your body to register that you've eaten enough food, so by eating too quickly it's very easy to overeat.

Here are some simple suggestions that you can try to help you get into the habit of eating a little slower:
- Put your knife and fork down between bites. The longer we hold our fork and knife in our hands, the more we are tempted to keep eating.
- Chew your food as much as you can. The longer you chew, the more your food breaks down and the easier it will be for your body to digest it. Chew thoroughly and pay attention to texture, taste and substance. Digestion actually starts in the mouth, so the more work you do here, the less you'll have to do in your stomach.

- Take a full breath in-between each mouthful. Not only does it give you an extra few seconds between bites but it also helps your entire body to relax.

## 2. Pay attention at meal times

Most bulimics eat with very little consciousness. They would rather shut off their mind than face the reality of the food they are eating. By not paying attention you can easily miss the comfortably full sensation that tells you to stop eating. This means you'll go straight to feeling overfull instead.

By paying attention you will really begin to notice food, how it affects your body and what it really tastes like. Paying attention will also really help you to understand the intimate relationship between food and your body. You will get a better understanding of what foods really satisfy your needs and how much you need to eat in order to feel comfortably full.

Helpful hints for paying attention to your food:
- When eating turn off the T.V, put the book down and instead just focus on the food. Sit down, remove all distractions and make it a pleasant, enjoyable experience. Perhaps try lighting a candle or playing some relaxing music.
- Tune into the physical sensations of eating food. Pay attention to the texture, tastes and aroma of the food. Notice how the taste of the food changes as you eat more of it. Notice how the food gets less tasty the more satisfied you become.
- Try eating all of your meals in one place. This will make your meal times more formal and allow you to create a new eating routine. When you're used to eating in just one place you'll be less likely to engage in future episodes of mindless "on the go" eating.
- Always put your food on a plate and sit down before starting to eat. By using a plate you are making your meal time official. You are signaling to yourself "I am having food now", instead of just grazing through snacks from the cupboard.

## Summary

Start to eat food mindfully. Begin to eat more slowly and pay attention to the physical sensation of eating food.

# Making Peace With Food Step 3:
## Tune into hunger

Due to chaotic eating habits our hunger tends to be erratic, scary, powerful and confusing. We don't trust our hunger, it's our worst enemy and we try to fight it as best we can. To recover from bulimia we need to make peace with our hunger. We need to become more aware of it, explore it, learn from it and start to get comfortable with it. In time this will heal our relationship with hunger.

As the relationship strengthens we can then trust and depend on our hunger as a reliable guide to how much, what and when we should eat (rather than following a dangerous restrictive diet). Using hunger as a guide is the secret key to lifelong recovery from bulimia (we will cover this in Stage 5 Intuitive Eating).

I want you to think of your hunger as a wild dog that hasn't really been looked after too well. Picture a dog that can be unpredictable, aggressive and furious at times. It's our job to tame that dog, to teach it that it has nothing to fear, and that it's okay to start trusting and even loving us. To do this we need to nurture, respect and care for the dog. Over time, if we do our job properly, our dog will learn how to be calm, gentle, reliable and trustworthy. Eventually our dog will stop being a scary wild animal and instead become our snuggly, trustworthy, loyal and loved pet.

To tune into hunger we need to start paying attention to our hunger signals throughout the day. The more we pay attention, the clearer and stronger the subtle hunger signals become.

## What you need to do:

### Step 1: Ask yourself "how hungry am I?"

Throughout the day I want you to mentally tune into your hunger and ask yourself "how hungry am I?" Then I want you to rate your hunger level by using the Hunger Scale.

**The Hunger Scale:**
1. Physically faint
2. Ravenous
3. Fairly hungry
4. Slightly hungry
5. Neutral
6. Pleasantly satisfied
7. Full
8. Over full
9. Bloated
10. Nauseous.

When using the hunger scale it's important to not let yourself get too hungry or you will make yourself prone to Physical Binge Urges. If possible try to keep yourself above "3. Fairly hungry". Also when eating try to avoid going above "7. Full" to avoid further risk of purging.

### Step 2: Ask yourself, "what does my hunger feel like?"

Everyone is unique and two people will not experience hunger in the exact same way. Although in general you can expect to experience at least a few of the following physical signs of hunger:

- Growling stomach.
- Light headedness.
- Difficulty concentrating.
- Irritability.
- Weakness and fatigue.
- Headaches.
- An empty insecure feeling.

- A hollow feeling in your stomach.
- Nausea.
- Shaking in your extremities.

This simple question will help you explore, learn and understand hunger sensations and feelings within your body.

### "How often should I do this?"
This only takes a few seconds to do, so please try to do this regularly throughout each day. It can be helpful to set your phone or watch to beep on the hour. Then when you hear the beep just take a few seconds to tune in and assess your hunger.

### "How long do I need to do this?"
For as long as you wish. It only takes a few seconds to do and it's a great habit as it will really help you to understand and trust your hunger.

### "Why does my hunger fluctuate so much from day to day?"
As you begin to get back in touch with your hunger you will start to notice that it fluctuates all the time. For no apparent reason you may be only slightly hungry one day, yet incredibly hungry the next. Your body is very complex and many factors can affect your level of hunger, such as:
- Exercise and physical activity levels
- What you ate previously
- A woman's menstrual cycle
- Genetics
- Muscle size
- Metabolism
- Amount and quality of sleep
- Alcohol consumption
- Mood and stress levels
- Drugs and medicines.

Sometimes there are no obvious reasons for day to day hunger fluctuations, but we must accept that changes in hunger levels are normal and trust that our body knows best. For many bulimics who have not learned to trust their hunger, this can be scary. They may feel greedy or out of control, when really they are just hungry.

Accept that daily and erratic hunger fluctuations are very natural and normal. When I was in recovery I would constantly say, "You know, eating this amount of food before would have classified as a binge, but now I know it's just hunger!" Very often I would say this after coming back from a session at the local gym. I knew the workout would make me more hungry than usual, so I trusted that my body knew best. I removed the limitations on how much she could acceptably eat in order to satisfy her true hunger. I knew it wasn't a binge urge; I was just more hungry than normal.

## Summary

When you ask yourself, "how hungry am I?" and "what does it feel like?" multiple times throughout the day, you will help yourself to reconnect with, understand and trust your hunger.

# Making Peace With Food:
## Super Short Version

If you need a quick recap, here is the super short version...

To help us make peace with food we want to get out of the habit of labelling foods as good and bad. Instead we want to label foods as "sometimes foods" and "all the time foods".

And, to help us overcome our harmful food rules, we can start adding portions of our favorite "sometimes" foods to our meal plan. Over time build up to including one or two portions of your "sometimes" foods in your meal plan every day.

By paying attention and eating slowly you can learn to understand, trust and deepen the relationship between your body and food.

You can also begin to become more intuitive with your hunger by asking "How hungry am I and what does it feel like?" multiple times throughout the day. This will help you to reconnect with, understand and trust your hunger.

# Stephanie's Success Story

" I really thought there was something wrong with me. That there was something wrong with my brain. I would binge and purge any chance I had. Any time I was alone at my apartment. I felt like a drug addict with food being my drug of choice.

After graduating from college I decided that I really needed to focus on recovery so I tried other recovery programs online. Many were depressing and wanted me to subscribe to online therapy. Many claimed it would take months or years for me to get better. They were reinforcing my fears that I was born with something wrong with my brain and therapy would need to fix it.

I had first discovered bulimiahelp.org when I was at my lowest. After reading through the book everything started to make sense I felt finally "this is something I can handle".

The book showed me I wasn't eating enough and it explained exactly what proportions of fats, carbs, and protein I should be eating which completely changed the way I prepared my meals. In no time I found I felt full after every meal; something that had never happened to me before. The book also provides other tips besides eating habits to help. It helped me understand why I felt so tired unless I had a b/p high. What I really like about it is that it's all step by step and really easy to understand. Better still, I didn't have to move onto the next step until I felt ready!

Of course I wasn't perfect, I still thought about food a lot and I would still b/p every so often. But the important thing was that I was making progress. For anyone nervous about weight gain, I actually lost weight, I'm not bloated anymore and I stopped having stomach aches.

So where am I now? Well I don't want to put a label on it...I don't want to say "I am cured" because then if I ever did b/p again I would label myself a failure. All I know is that I look at food completely differently now. I see it as fuel for my body so I can do the things I want to do in life! Instead of having to spend my time whenever I am alone bingeing and purging I do a lot of other things. I paint, play with my dog, go hiking, play basketball. These are all things I felt too tired to do before and now I feel energetic and look forward to doing them. Thank you so much bulimiahelp.org! "

-Stephanie

# Stage 4 in Recovery: Self Acceptance

For this stage in recovery, I am going to hand you over to Catherine Liberty. In 2008 Catherine followed the Bulimia Help Method to overcome bulimia. She then joined us in 2011 to work as a qualified Recovery Coach and now dedicates her time helping others achieve their freedom from bulimia.

Over to you Catherine....

Although I've been recovered and working as a recovery coach for many years now, I still remember my own struggles with negative body image as if they happened yesterday. I suppose the memory of having to endure such pain and misery never really leaves you.

Like many people, I spent the majority of my life in the pursuit of genuine happiness, but unfortunately, I got it all wrong. Rather than allowing my passions and talents to flourish, and rather than striving to become the best version of myself that I could be, I chose to pour all of my time and energy into achieving the "thin ideal". After all, everywhere we look we're sold the idea that thinness and beauty equates to happiness and success. How was I supposed to know I'd been lied to all along?

Restriction featured heavily throughout my life, and ultimately led me to develop bulimia and an even more warped perception of self. Even as a very young child I dieted in an attempt to silence the bullies who mocked my weight and appearance and there was a time in my life when I genuinely believed that being thinner would make me a better person. I thought it would make me more worthy of love and acceptance. I thought it would make me special. I thought it would make me happy.

Up until the time when I started my recovery at Bulimia Help, I honestly had no memory of ever being comfortable or happy in my own skin. I had always been at war with my body and for many years the idea of trying to recover while also hating myself was unfathomable. How was I supposed to deal with even more weight changes? How could I just relinquish control like that? How could I give up on my "dream" of being thin and perfect?

When it came to recovery, like most people, I had a lot of huge concerns. I had such a painfully negative view of myself that I was reluctant to allow it to get any worse. But that's the trouble when you harbor misconceptions about recovery. You convince yourself that in order to recover you're going to have to spend the rest of your life feeling disgusted with your body and feeling totally devastated every time you look in the mirror. After all, if you can never remember a point in your life when you even remotely liked yourself, how do you even begin to imagine a future where you will?

It's confusing to live in a world where it is more acceptable to hate yourself than it is to love yourself. We read statements such as "roughly two thirds of adults suffer from negative body image" (Algers, et al, 2009) or "60% of adults admitting that they actually feel ashamed of the way they look" (Centre for Appearance Research, 2012) and we think sure, that's understandable, everyone hates something about themselves, right? And it's true. Even the most well-adjusted people experience negative thoughts about themselves from time to time. It's impossible to feel good about yourself all of the time and that's not something we're striving for in recovery. But when the way you feel about your body or your life stands in the way of daily functioning, success, and happiness, it's a sign that something is drastically wrong and that you need to make a change.

## "What's the difference between a positive, and a negative body image?"

In essence, the term "body image" refers to the way we think and feel about our own physical selves and attractiveness, and it can also encompass the way we imagine others perceive our physical beauty.

### Positive Body Image

We have a positive body image when we are able to accept our body as it is. When we feel happy in our own skin, and have a realistic perception of our size. A big part of positive body image also involves the understanding that physical appearance has nothing to do with our intrinsic value as a person, that there is no one ideal body type, and that many different shapes and sizes can be both healthy and attractive. Someone with a healthy body image may still experience negative thoughts about themselves from time to time, but they will not base their sense of self-esteem on their shape, size or weight.

### Negative Body Image

When we suffer from a negative body image we often have a distorted perception of our physical size and shape. We believe that our size is a direct indication of our worth and we feel totally inadequate when comparing ourselves to those around us. Someone with a negative body image will base their sense of self-esteem almost exclusively on their shape, size, or weight.

## Body Image Distortion

As if having a negative body image wasn't bad enough, many people with bulimia also suffer from a condition known as "Body image distortion" (or BID for short). When you suffer from BID the image you see in the mirror, and the size you truly believe your body to be, can be massively distorted when compared with reality. As you can imagine, a distorted body image tends to cancel out all objective reality too, meaning that you will continue to feel fat, even when you're not. When the image reflected back to you in the mirror is distorted, then no amount of logic or reassurance will ever be able to convince you of your true size.

Researchers have found that people with bulimia tend to significantly overestimate their own body size (Mohra et al, 2011) while some studies have even gone on to suggest that when you develop bulimia, your brain can start to process body image in an entirely different way (Eynde, et al, 2011). But one thing a lot of people don't realize is that BID and misconception of your own body size can actually be caused by malnutrition and restrictive eating (remember that purging is interpreted in the same way by your body as restricting). This helps to explain why most people find their negative-body image resolving naturally, over time, during their recovery (more on that in a second).

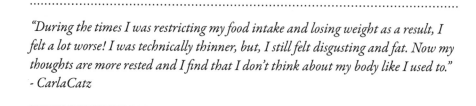

*"During the times I was restricting my food intake and losing weight as a result, I felt a lot worse! I was technically thinner, but, I still felt disgusting and fat. Now my thoughts are more rested and I find that I don't think about my body like I used to."*
*- CarlaCatz*

So as crazy as this sounds, the best way to feel thinner and happier is to stop restricting and to allow yourself to reach your natural healthy set point weight.

And here's another surprising thing you may not realize about recovery...

**You do NOT have to love yourself (or your body) in order to recover!**

I remember feeling so frustrated with myself early on in recovery. "If only I could be happy with my body, then I would finally be able to stop," I would say. So many people are under the impression that in order to recover from bulimia, they first have to make peace with their body, or somehow learn to love themselves. But I am here to tell you right now that this is just not true. You do NOT have to love your body in order to recover from bulimia. You do NOT even have to like your body, or yourself, in order to begin this process. It actually works the other way around. First you must work on your recovery, and then gradually, over time, you will be rewarded with a natural boost in body-image and self-esteem.

**"You mean my body-image issues will resolve all on their own?"**

Yes. Once you stop binge eating and purging and begin eating in a healthy, balanced way, many biological and physiological changes will occur in your body. Your brain chemistry will start to normalize, your hormone levels will balance out, and you'll overcome nutritional deficiencies. As a direct result of these changes, the amount of body-negativity you experience will decrease and your obsessive thought patterns will diminish (Fairburn, Marcus, et al., 1993). Your body image will come into alignment with objective reality, and any distress caused by previously negative body image should dissipate (Stefanie Lein, 2014).

Then, as you continue to thrive in your recovery and constantly find yourself doing "the impossible" you will begin to experience feelings of accomplishment, success, and pride, that have nothing to do with your weight or body. As a result you'll boost your self-esteem and feelings of self-worth in healthy, productive ways, and you'll feel further empowered to abandon self-hatred and destructive behaviors once and for all.

At a certain point in your recovery you will know without a doubt that any body type, any body size, and any future changes to your body are worth it if you can keep living bulimia-free forever. Recovery really is that good.

**But these changes do take time. They can not happen overnight.**
Even when you're doing everything right and pouring your heart and soul into your recovery, improvements to your body image and feelings of self-worth will still need time to manifest. Realistically you're going to need to wait for at least 6 months, and maybe a little longer, for those natural improvements to take effect. I know that seems like such a long time right now, but keep the bigger picture in mind. Really, it's only a tiny fraction of your life. You can do this.

So that means for the time being, and especially in those first few months of recovery, the self-loathing may well continue. Some people even find it gets a little worse before it gets better, and if that happens to you I want you to try really hard to not panic. It is a temporary challenge, it is a normal part of the recovery process, and it will pass.

If you allow your negative thoughts to catalyse into self-destructive behaviors (like choosing to restrict when you experience fat thoughts, or consciously deciding to purge after a meal because you are feeling bloated) then they will only ever serve to keep you trapped and miserable. But, if you can work hard to accept negative thoughts and fat feelings as a natural part of life for now, then you will drastically reduce your body anxiety levels.

# Accepting Negative Thoughts

Do you remember those reflection and acceptance statements Richard shared with us earlier in the book? Well, they can be applied to any uncomfortable feelings about your body too. So whenever you're experiencing an overwhelmingly negative thought, comfort and reassure yourself by saying: "It's okay to be uncomfortable right now." and "I can handle these feelings."

Learning to embrace your discomfort may feel counter-intuitive, after all, you are here to heal, you are here to recover, and you are here because you desperately want to make peace with your body. But trust me on this one, when you can get to a place in your life where you've cultivated a true attitude of acceptance, everything will change for the better. Your negative, self-hating thoughts are not special. Stop giving them attention and they will weaken.

*"I used to think that if I beat myself up enough it would motivate me to be better. Unfortunately, I think that plan backfired! Self-destructive thoughts lead to self-destructive behaviors, depression, hopelessness, and the feeling that you never will be enough.*

*It wasn't until I actually accepted myself, flaws and all, that I began to blossom into the person I had wanted to force myself to be through self-abuse. The painful irony of it! I'm still not perfect but now I look in the mirror and I see a woman who is strong, creative, loving, and has many good things to offer the world. I see the positives, rather than the negatives. I hope that you can start to see how beautiful you really are! Let go of your self-depreciation and embrace your imperfections, your originality!" - Diana*

## Reframe negative self-talk into honest, but empowering, self-talk

You know what it's like when those bulimic thoughts take over. They tear you apart, they magnify your inner critic, and they blind you to your true achievements.

Even when you've been in recovery for some time, there can be those moments where it feels impossible to praise yourself. You may feel unworthy of the attention and you may find it hard to believe that your achievements are anything special.

Let's get one thing straight right now... you are not your looks and you are not your eating disorder. You are far more than the eye can see. You are your culture and your history. You are your individual quirks and unique talents. You are your spirit, your sense of humour, and your zest for life. You are infused by the traits and wisdom of all of the people you have ever known and loved. You are a miracle of life.

Just because you may be feeling miserable about your body right now it does not mean that you automatically have to feel miserable about your life too. In fact you may only feel this way right now because you're basing all of your self-worth on the size and shape of your body. Instead, from this moment on, I want you to strive to redefine your measures of success.

When we fixate on our bodies so much it seems like nothing else matters, but by pushing ourselves to consider our true values, and by realizing that we are unique human beings with endless opportunities and talents, we encourage a shift in the negative mindset.

Start to actively notice personal traits, talents and achievements that transcend your physical appearance. Realize that success, happiness and stability cannot be achieved through body size and look to alternative measures of your worth.

The following exercises are wonderful and can be used at any stage of recovery.

## My Positive List

Grab a piece of paper and at the top write "My Positive List".

- Now make a list of the following:
- Anything that you are proud of.
- Positive changes you've experienced in recovery.
- Things you like about yourself.
- Positive statements a close friend or loved one might use to describe you.
- What makes you unique and special.
- Things you are good at.

- Aspects of your personality that you like.
- Anything at all that makes you feel more positive.

The longer the list is, the better. Then, whenever you are in need of a self-esteem boost, read over the list.

You may find this exercise uncomfortable or silly to begin with, but this is a very normal defensive reaction. Give it a chance anyway; you may be surprised by how beneficial it is to your recovery.

## Positive Self-Talk

When struggling with a negative body image we really can be our own worst critics. We subject ourselves to a torrent of verbal and emotional abuse on a daily basis, and our self-esteem and happiness further erodes as a result. Luckily, you can begin to disrupt the cycle of negative self-talk by instead focusing on cultivating more positive self-talk.

You may be wondering if positive self-talk conflicts with emotional acceptance, but I assure you that it doesn't. In fact, acknowledging and accepting your thoughts and emotional state is the first step towards reframing any negative self-talk that you're experiencing. In essence, positive self-talk is all about learning to be kinder to yourself by striving to accept, but ultimately to redefine what it is that you're experiencing, all the while keeping it in its original, emotional context. For example, if your original pattern of negative self-talk was "I hate myself for gaining weight, I am weak and disgusting!" Then upon noticing this pattern of negative self-talk you would strive to reframe it in a kinder, more logical way. So "I hate myself for gaining weight, I am weak and disgusting!" could become "I feel so disappointed and uncomfortable with this weight gain, but I know that weight fluctuations are part of the process. I am strong for choosing recovery, I just need to give my body a little more time to adjust."

If you find yourself saying "My stomach is SO fat and disgusting!" you could strive to change this to "I am overwhelmed by the bloating I'm experiencing right now, but bloating is temporary and a very important step towards healing. I am becoming healthier each day."

Negative self-talk such as "I am weak and can not control my weight without bulimia!" can change to "I feel weak right now, but I know that purging was never the answer. My metabolism needs time to heal and by choosing recovery today I am giving myself the opportunity to have a bright and happy future."

I must stress: this is not about striving to "think happy thoughts" because as you know by now, we really don't have much control over our thoughts. It is about applying mature and logical reasoning to any abusive or hurtful self-talk. It is about accepting and honoring the fact that you feel terrible, disappointed, fat, or ashamed, but then striving to break free from those patterns of negative self-talk regardless. It is about learning to treat yourself with the love and compassion that you truly deserve.

It's very important that you are honest with your self-talk, as researchers, from the University of Waterloo and the University of New Brunswick found that people with low self-esteem actually felt worse after repeating generically positive (but untrue) statements about themselves. So this is not about trying to lie to yourself by saying things like "I love my body unconditionally" when you're feeling really fat. It's about acknowledging your true emotional state in a less abusive manner and striving to comfort yourself with the facts of the situation.

Psychologist and life coach, Dr. Suzanne Gelb explains:
"Affirmations need to be scripted with total honesty in order for them to work. They need to be honest, self-respecting assessments about where we're at, what we're learning, and what we're capable of becoming. They are affirmations of truth—and the truth will set you free."

So the next time you find yourself being critical or speaking harshly to yourself, encourage more positive self-talk by:

1. Acknowledge what it is that you're feeling.
2. Encourage yourself to look at the bigger picture and focus on logic and the facts of the situation.
3. Show yourself the kindness and respect that you would show to a friend.

Even if you do not feel an immediate difference when engaging in more positive self-talk, give it some time, and you will see your negative thoughts becoming more balanced and less critical. You will begin to perceive yourself in a new light and your entire outlook on life and recovery will change as a result.

# Create a Recovery Environment

If you're serious about your recovery then it's time to commit to banishing as many negative influences from your life as you possibly can. When your home (and your life) is recovery-friendly, you'll be actively limiting your exposure to potential triggers and you'll feel far more resilient when unavoidable triggers do come up.

Here are some tips for creating a healthy recovery environment that will promote lasting change:

## Have a technology clear out.

Remove the calorie counting and goal weight apps from your phone, delete any triggering bookmarks from your computer, and send any "thinspo" images straight to your recycle bin. If you're following celebrities on social media who trigger negative thoughts then hit that unfollow button. Basically make a point of deleting and removing anything that is not recovery-friendly from your phone, computer, and tablet.

If you're suddenly left with a huge void you can replace those things with recovery-friendly versions. Bookmark some recovery websites, save inspirational images, follow former bulimics and recovery champions on social media, search for apps that will promote health and healing.

## Throw away magazines and consider changing your TV viewing habits.

Studies at Stanford University and the University of Massachusetts reported that seventy percent of college women feel worse about how they look after reading women's magazines and in 2012, the Centre for Appearance Research found that 70% of adult women and 40% of adult men felt pressure from television and magazines to have a perfect body.

It's also worth noting that even when you're fully aware that the images you're being exposed to do not match reality, they can still have a negative impact on you. Research suggests that more than one third of young women continue to aspire to look like the models they see in advertisements even when they are aware of airbrushing and the unrealistic nature of those advertisements (Pretty as a picture, CREDOS, 2011).

Reducing your exposure to these unnecessary life triggers will leave you feeling less pressured and less prone to negative body image. You do not need magazines or triggering TV shows in your life, there is so much more to live for!

## Get rid of your "skinny" clothes.

The start of recovery is the best time to clear out your old clothing. I know it's hard, especially if you've held onto these clothes for quite some time with the dream of one day fitting into them. But now it is time to let go. Holding on to those things will only keep your negative body image alive. So be brave, take a stand and donate any old "skinny" clothes to your local charity shop or homeless shelter. It's good for you and it's good for your community.

## Commit to avoiding toxic conversations, situations, and people.

No matter where you are or who you are with, you do not have to participate in triggering conversations, and avoiding them will be good for your recovery. So from this point on, refuse to engage in topics relating to weight-loss, body shaming, fat talk or anything else that you find especially triggering.

- If a conversation becomes toxic you could leave the room to "make a call" or to get a drink or visit the bathroom.
- Think of 2-3 topics or conversation changers that you can use next time you find people trying to include you in their toxic conversations. Maybe there is a story you read about in the news that you'd like to share? Perhaps you had an interesting experience at work that you can talk about?
- Think about the kinds of people you are surrounded by. Are they positive, strong people with depth and integrity? Do they make you feel like a better person and offer nurturing friendships? I am in no way saying that people who engage in diet or fat talk are inherently bad, or that they need to be avoided. I am just saying that you deserve to be surrounded by wonderful people who can support you in your recovery whether they know about your bulimia or not.

# Set Some Body "Checking" Limits

Bulimia makes us extremely paranoid and self-conscious when it comes to our outward appearance, so much so that many of us find ourselves engaging in checking behaviors multiple times each day. The trouble with this is that when you're constantly feeling your stomach, or scrutinizing your appearance in a full length mirror in an attempt to alleviate your body anxieties, you are only feeding the obsession. More checking always means more negative body image.

**What you need to do:**
1.  Try to think of your most problematic checking behaviors and list them. Making a list may not seem especially productive, but awareness is the first step towards breaking free from damaging habits. Do you feel your stomach after meals? Do you weigh yourself immediately after purging?
2.  Next, outline some checking limits. If you're drawn to pat your stomach after every meal, challenge yourself to do this just once or twice through the day at first, rather than after everything you've eaten. If you scrutinize your body in a full length mirror at the start of each day, become aware of how long you typically spend at the mirror and challenge yourself to cut that time in half. If you weigh yourself multiple times each day, try to limit this as much as possible. Helpful practical steps can include repositioning mirrors, or adding a post-it or sticker to remind yourself to avoid checking your body and removing the scales from your bathroom, and so on.

When you self-impose limits like this you are actively reducing the amount of time you would usually spend agonizing over the way you look and you should definitely find it helps you to reduce your negative thought processes. Of course this doesn't mean that you should avoid looking in the mirror or looking at your body altogether, it's just about breaking free from the "need" to check on a regular basis.

# Common Challenges:
## I can't stop weighing myself!

If you are weighing yourself constantly, to a point where it is causing anxiety, then you may want to consider getting rid of your scales. You don't need them and they won't help with recovery. This includes any other weight measurement tools you may have too, such as your "skinny clothes" or measuring tapes. You will not need them to measure your progress. Your improved wellbeing, confidence and energy levels will let you know that you are on the path to recovery. By looking after yourself and your body in the best way you can, your weight/size will be at the healthiest level that is possible for your natural body type.

Scales are one of the biggest binge triggers. It's been proven that both good and bad scale numbers can lead to bingeing. If we get on the scale and it says that we have lost a great deal of weight, we can use that as a justification to overindulge. If the scale says we have not done as well as we had hoped, we can use that as the reason to quit and give up.

Scales are not accurate. Studies show a fluctuation of plus or minus 1kg ( 2.2lbs) over consecutive days is common, and fluctuations of plus or minus 0.5kg (1lbs) are very common. Weight can fluctuate and vary depending on hormone changes, gains in lean muscle mass, water retention, and even whether or not you've used the restroom recently. So it's definitely time to ditch the scales!

..............................................................................................

*"I didn't think I could ever get rid of my scale! I used to weigh myself before and after each binge/purge, every morning and night. When I first stopped throwing everything up, I still weighed myself every day and after a few days, I actually lost weight. Then I got so obsessed with keeping that weight off, I panicked at gaining even as little as 200g. That's like a glass of water. Wow, it sounds really stupid now, getting upset over that but stepping on the scales only made me start binge/purge again. I didn't think I could stop stepping on the scale, but after a day or two, I finally did it! I took out the batteries and hid them in the back of my closet. (I was too cheap to throw out a perfectly working scale).*

*Now I can eat a "normal" meal, and since I don't have to weigh myself, it feels like a huge weight has been lifted off my shoulders. If any of you are reading this and feeling hesitant toward throwing out your scales, I say do it!! It's the biggest thing that I've done physically to help me start my recovery!!!" - Little Cat*

## Tips for ditching the scales

- If you can't throw them out, try hiding your scales instead.
- If you do feel that you must check in with a scale, try not to weigh in any more than once every two weeks. Over time as your confidence builds, increase the period of time between checking in.
- If your doctor needs to record your weight explain that the numbers can be upsetting and ask to step on the scales backwards. This may seem a little strange to you, but any doctor will totally understand your request. Remember it is vital that you put your recovery first.
- Eventually, when you feel strong enough to live without the scales, rejoice in your new found freedom!

*"The last time my therapist and husband told me to get rid of my scale, I had an all out panic attack. So my husband hid it in the garage. I found it and convinced him to give it back. He did and now I've started obsessing on it again. Well, tonight's trash night and I handed it my husband and watched him walk it to the trash can by the road. I'm scared and relieved at the same time. I know it's a trigger and it had to go". - Anonymous Coaching Member*

*"Many people in recovery worry that if they stop weighing themselves, their weight will spiral out of control. There actually is no correlation between weighing regularly and maintaining a healthy weight. The number on the scale does not show your recovery progress, and it doesn't indicate how healthy you are. There really is no good reason for weighing yourself in recovery. Spare yourself the emotional rollercoaster of weighing, and get rid of that scale once and for all!"*
*- Jen Knaebel, Bulimia Help Recovery Coach*

# Common Challenges:
# "I don't know who I am without bulimia?"

It's natural to experience a sense of loss of identity when you begin your recovery. After all, bulimia and disordered eating may be all you've ever known and all you've defined yourself by. But as you continue on your journey you're going to find old and new interests once more. You're going to discover your true strengths and talents, and you are going to achieve so many things that were not possible before recovery. That's not to say that life will be perfect, because we all have our struggles and challenges, but it will be infinitely better.

If you're struggling to discover who you are without bulimia, consider the following: What is the one thing you've always wanted to do in your life? What makes you stand out from the crowd? What would you like to do with the precious time you have now that you're not spending your days bingeing and purging? Take some time to reflect on this, some answers may be obvious, and that's great. Others may take more time to become apparent, and that's okay too. There's no need to rush this. Just remember that you can do anything. You can be anything. It is never too late to become the greatest version of yourself.

When I think about all of the changes that I have made in my life over the past five years it still overwhelms me. I went from being a fragile little girl who never believed recovery from bulimia would be possible to someone who now feels like a true champion in her heart. I have transformed myself completely. I have removed myself from a lifetime of pain, self-loathing and hatred and created the new me. The new me is strong, grateful, inspired and free but also vulnerable sometimes too. I think liberated is the best word to describe how I feel today, in honesty it's how I feel every day since I removed bulimia from my life.

Changing the way you feel about yourself and losing that desire to lose weight or achieve the perfect body will take time. It's a process. So for now just keep focusing on your freedom and keep discovering how incredible life can be once bulimia is out of the picture. I promise you that the way you feel about your body right now is not going to be the way you feel about it at the end of this journey. Take things slowly, take as many proactive steps as you can, and appreciate that a transformation of this magnitude is going to take time.

# Self Acceptance:
## Super Short Version

If you need a quick recap, here is the super short version...

- You do not have to like your body, or yourself in order to recover from bulimia.
- First you must work on your recovery and then gradually, over time, you will be rewarded with a natural boost in body-image and self-esteem.
- The best way to feel thinner and happier is to stop restricting and to allow yourself to reach your natural healthy set point weight.
- Realistically you're going to need to wait for at least 6 months (maybe a little longer) for those natural improvements to take effect.

The next time you find yourself being critical or speaking harshly to yourself, encourage more positive self-talk by:
1. Acknowledge what it is that you're feeling.
2. Encourage yourself to look at the bigger picture and focus on logic and the facts of the situation.
3. Show yourself the kindness and respect that you would show to a friend.

- Make a list of all your positive attributes and refer to it regularly.
- Commit to banishing as many negative influences from your life as you possibly can.
- Try to gradually limit the number of times you are body checking daily.
- Stop weighing yourself (it really doesn't help).

# Julie's Success Story

" After almost a decade of having bulimia with anorexic tendencies I had pretty much given up all hope of being able to have a healthy relationship with food. Almost every meal, (or non-meal) created havoc in my mind which was nearly always in overdrive. I am now, on the most part, a happy and healthy eater.

My bulimic lifestyle was so chaotic, it took over so much of my life, so much time, it caused so much anxiety, and produced so much unhappiness. I tried counseling, medication and a short stay in inpatient, but nothing ever worked!

I'd just think "this is not working" and lose all hope when I didn't see any kind of change to begin with. I'd give it my all for a few days but the overwhelming urge to binge and purge was just too strong.

Every situation seemed like an opportunity to binge. An empty house, a cancelled date, a "buy one get one free" offer at the shops.

For so long I didn't want to acknowledge my eating disorder. If I didn't think about it then I didn't have it. I could still work as a health professional full time, from 9-6 (with a very small, if any, lunch) and no one at work would suspect a thing. Then I'd come home and as fast as possible buy, eat and purge. Then get rid of all the evidence and sit down like it never happened.

So although I'm proud of my recovery, I'm so used to blocking out so many feelings and emotions, that I find it hard to acknowledge what I have achieved. I hope this makes sense!

The main reason I'm writing this is to give anyone reading this hope. I really believe if I can do this then we all can. I know I used to hear about other recovered people and think 'I'll never do it, I'm not like them, I couldn't give this up.' But I have and I so strongly believe we all can. But sometimes you have to reach rock bottom to start climbing back up!

I was so sick of being sick. I had had enough of this disease. I really hope and believe you all can end your fight with eating disorders too.
Thank you Bulimia Help!"

– Julie

# Stage 5 in Recovery: Intuitive Eating

We have now reached the final stage of The Bulimia Help Method recovery program. This is where everything comes together to ensure your recovery is rock solid and lifelong. This is where all of your commitment and dedication to recovery really pays off. This is the final hurdle on your journey to ultimate freedom for life.

At this stage, if you have been following the steps in the book, you should have been doing structured eating for a while now. This was your building block that helped you to re-learn healthy and normal eating, but as we know, this type of eating is not realistic or healthy for anyone to adhere to forever. Eating cannot (and should not) be that "perfect" and inflexible.

So what do we replace structured eating with? We can't go back to how we used to eat. It was our old eating habits that got us into trouble in the first place. We also need to avoid anything involving diet plans, rules and restrictions. What we need is a new frame of reference to guide us on how we should eat food. One without any pain, suffering, rules or plans.

Let me introduce you to Intuitive Eating. This is the process where you listen to your hunger cues to guide you as to what, when and how much you should eat. It's an extremely powerful and simple way to eat food that will enable you to maintain a healthy weight for life.  I believe Intuitive Eating to be the secret key to total recovery for life.

I must stress that this is a very advanced stage of recovery. It is important that you have successfully mastered structured eating and made peace with food before you attempt to become an intuitive eater. If you are below your most healthy weight range and/or still experiencing disordered eating, your body will not be able to give accurate information about the right amount or type of food it needs. Many of our members find that they are not truly ready to embrace this stage until they have been using structured eating for 6-12 months (in some cases even a little longer than this).

Only move on to this step when you can answer "yes" to the following questions:

- Have you used structured eating successfully for a number of months?
- Have you overcome your fear and anxiety of all foods?
- Have you stopped restricting?
- Have you overcome your primal hunger?
- Have you overcome your malnutrition?
- Have you stopped bingeing and purging?
- Have your subtle sensations of hunger and satiety returned?

If you feel ready to become an intuitive eater, give it a go. However, if Intuitive Eating starts to feel too difficult then there is no harm in sticking with structured eating for a little longer. Continue to work on developing peace with food and work on strengthening your hunger awareness. There is no rush here. Remember, we are aiming for total recovery for life. If you feel that you are not quite ready, it's still a good idea to read through this section so that you can get a good understanding of what it's all about.

## Eating the way nature intended.

The human species is the pinnacle of evolution, the most intelligent and sophisticated animal in the known universe. Do you think Mother Nature would have overlooked the simple matter of guiding us as to what to eat, how much to eat, and when to eat? How do you think wild animals and human beings have survived over millions of years? How did our ancestors survive without supermarkets, diets, and nutritionists? Our ancestors didn't even know what calories or vitamins were, they just used their intuition.

Think about someone who doesn't struggle with his or her weight. If you're having trouble thinking of someone like that, think of a baby or a young child. They just seem to know when, what and how much food they need. When their body needs fuel, they get hungry and they respond to this hunger by eating. Then, they simply stop eating when their hunger is satisfied, even if there is food left on their plate.

Most of them really enjoy food and seem to be able to eat whatever they want. However, they'll turn down even the most delicious food if they aren't hungry. They listen to their body, are in charge of their choices, and do whatever feels right for them at the time. This is called "Intuitive Eating".

Intuitive eating is based on the premise that becoming more attuned to your body's natural hunger signals is a more effective way to attain a healthy weight for life than any diet or food plan. It's a process that helps you to create a healthy relationship with food by encouraging you to pay more attention to mind and body cues. Intuitive Eating goes by many other names such as "non-dieting", "the non-diet approach", "normal eating", "wisdom eating", "conscious eating" and more.

### How do we lose our intuition?

When you were born, food was just food. You cried when you were hungry and stopped eating when you were full. You never thought about weight issues and you never had a weight problem. You used your internal regulator called "hunger" to know very clearly when and how much you should eat and you were 100% instinctive when doing so.

Unfortunately this didn't last for long as you grew up in our diet obsessed culture. Like a sponge soaking up water, you began to absorb the diet rules, the faulty thin myths and a fear of fat. Everywhere we look in our media there are messages about losing weight. It's like a huge avalanche of weight loss promotion that plays over and over and over again. It doesn't take long for all of this information to sink in and do damage. For example, in one study school children showed a stronger aversion to being overweight than to being blind or physically disabled; even children as young as 8 are restricting their food intake and by the age of 15 one in three have been on a diet. As we grow up we lose touch with our natural sensations of hunger and satiety.

We stop asking ourselves "Am I hungry?" and "What am I hungry for?" and instead we rely on the time of day, the calorie or fat content of food, and even our mood to dictate how much we should eat. Western society guides us away from our natural instincts and we quickly forget how to be intuitive eaters.

**The only way we can truly know what we need to eat.**

It's madness to think that some expert in a white coat, or any form of diet plan, can know your exact energy needs and how much food you, as an individual, need to maintain optimal health. Diet plans do not take your genetic makeup into account, they are incapable of calculating your daily energy expenditure, and they have no clue as to what your basic metabolic rate is. They cannot account for natural changes in your day to day hunger levels and your everyday lifestyle changes. A diet may tells us that we can only have 1 egg white on 1 slice toast for breakfast, however what happens if we eat this but we are still feeling hungry and getting cravings for another slice of toast or perhaps a sausage? The answer is that it can lead to a binge! The only way we can truly know what we need to eat is to listen to our own hunger and intuitive cues. Your intuition knows what your body needs better than any diet in the world.

**Intuitive Eating helps to prevent overeating.**

Most people in western society do not pay attention to their hunger and instead rely on external cues for when to eat. They may eat because:

- It's time to eat.
- The food is there and looks tasty.
- They feel bored.
- They want to numb negative emotions.
- They worry they will become hungry later in the day.
- They were taught that they must clear their plate.

All of these cues have one major problem: they do not take into account whether or not you are actually hungry! If you don't listen to your natural signals of hunger and fullness then it becomes very easy to eat more food than you actually need. By far the most common reason for unnecessary weight gain in western culture is constant overeating. This is because in our society we are told we should fear our hunger, rather than listen to it. If we continue to ignore our intuitive hunger and fullness cues after a while they just wither away and we will end up eating more than we need simply because we don't realize we are full.

If we listen to our hunger and satiety we can eat an amount of food that is perfect for us. Even if we eat a little too much, or not enough at a meal, that's perfectly okay. The next time, our hunger levels will naturally adjust to take that into account. This helps us to avoid overeating and allows us to easily and happily maintain our natural healthy weight for life.

Sounds too good to be true? A study of nearly 1300 college women by Tracy Tylka from Ohio State University found that intuitive eaters are more optimistic, have better self-esteem and a lower body mass index (BMI) without internalizing culture's unrealistically thin ideal.

### I know lots about nutrition, why do I need intuition?

After countless diets, counting calories and food obsessions, bulimics tend to know more about nutrition than most people do, but just knowing about nutrition isn't good enough. If nutritional knowledge was all that was needed to be a healthy eater, then bulimics would be some of the healthiest eaters on the planet. Obviously nutritional knowledge alone does not work.

The problem is that our nutritional knowledge has overtaken our intuitive knowledge. We put too much focus on nutrition and we ignore what we really feel like eating. This can make us feel deprived. By ignoring our intuition we are ignoring our internal hunger signals and dulling the relationship between us and our body. This doesn't work in the long run. We need to push away the nutritional guidelines and instead start to use our intuition.

### But I am scared, intuitive eating feels like I am losing control.

It can feel like we are losing control but lets look at the following examples

Example 1: Lucy eats what she wants when she feels like it, she does not count calories or fat grams, she eats when she is hungry and stops eating when she is full. She is at her natural set point and doesn't worry about her weight.

Example 2: Jenny obsesses about food. She continually counts calories and restricts her food intake. Jenny also tries to keep away from 'bad' foods yet finds she can't. This leads to binge eating. Afterwards Jenny feels really guilty so purges to regain control. She is constantly obsessed with her weight.

Who has more control? Lucy or Jenny? Hopefully the correct answer is pretty obvious.

## Why are diets so tempting?

Diets can be tempting because you don't have to think for yourself. It takes the pressure off deciding what to eat. But the problem is that dieting leads straight back to an eating disorder. We need to start thinking for ourselves and we need to make our own unique choices as to what we really want to eat.

*"YES YES YES. I sometimes STILL have the urge to hop on a diet, (for the security of feeling in control), then I realize I'm not in control - the diet is." - Amy*

## What is the difference between mindful and intuitive eating?

Mindful eating is the practice of eating slowly with awareness and using your senses, while intuitive eating is eating what you want, when you want it, based solely on hunger and fullness signals.

*"Even now I am still amazed that my body has this capability to tell me what it needs to eat, when it is hungry, when it is full. I spent my entire life bingeing on food and never really connecting to true hunger and satiety.*

*Long before I developed a recognized eating disorder I overate to block out the world. Even as a baby the doctors advised my parents to water down my milk because all I ever did was cry for more food, I mean can you believe that?! A whole lifetime of eating that way and I was still able to become an intuitive eater."*
*- Anna*

So let's get started with the first step to becoming an intuitive eater.

# Intuitive Eating Step 1:
# Eat What You Feel Like

In this step you are going to practice using your intuition to choose what you would like to eat. The real key to this stage is for you to eat what you feel like and not what you think you should eat.

**What you need to do:**
Choose one meal a day to begin the process. You can pick which one. For this meal don't plan what you are going to eat. Once you notice that you are becoming hungry, wrap your hands around your stomach and close your eyes for a moment and then ask yourself: **"What do I "feel" like eating?"**

Spend a few moments here. Give your intuition a little time to answer the question. Try to get a picture in your mind or imagine the taste of the food you are hungry for.

It's important you ask "what do I FEEL like eating?" and not "what do I WANT to eat?" These are two different questions and they can have two very different answers. By asking "what do I FEEL like?" you ensure you are eating foods that you are really craving. If you ask yourself "what do I WANT to eat?" you might bypass your intuition and instead choose a food based on how healthy you think it is.

Make sure you let yourself eat what you FEEL like eating. Is cake and ice cream calling to you? Go for it! Fancy a bit of pasta? As long as you're actually hungry and feeling like it... then go for it! Allow yourself to eat exactly what you are craving, no matter what the food is. Give yourself full permission to eat the food, guilt free. Take your time, eat with awareness and notice how eating what you really feel like is very satisfying.

Don't worry if you don't always know what you feel like eating. This is very normal. There will be lots of times when your intuition does not indicate a clear preference as to what your body wants to eat. At these times, when you don't know what you 'feel' like eating, it is best to choose an "all the time" food rather than a "sometimes" food.

To start with, you may want to apply this to just a few meals throughout the week and build up gradually from there.

## FAQs

### "But I don't want to eat the food I am craving!"

It's important not to deny yourself the food that you really want. It's okay to crave a "sometimes food". It might be 8am in the morning and you are craving doughnuts for breakfast. If you have a thought such as, "I don't need that doughnut," consider the possibility that by eating the doughnut you will be satisfied and not haunted by a craving. Think about it. As soon as you tell yourself not to eat a certain food, you upset the natural balance in your relationship with it, so rather than wanting it less, that "forbidden food" becomes more attractive. From this day forward, nothing is off-limits to you.

### "What if I just want to eat chocolate all the time?"

This is a common misconception. In fact the exact opposite happens. Just because you may have felt like eating chocolate all day long before recovery, doesn't mean that it will happen now.

Food habituation research shows that the more a person is exposed and allowed to eat a food, the less desirable it becomes to them over time. Food habituation has been demonstrated in many species (including humans) and with many foods, including: pizza, chocolate and potato chips. If you can have something any time you want, it stops being so special. If a kid can play with any toy except a blue truck, have a guess as to which toy he will want to play with. Whereas if the kid plays with the blue truck every day, he won't find it as special. If you can have chocolate whenever you want it, eventually it will become about as exciting as an apple.

### "So, if I feel like eating some cheesecake, are you saying I should eat cheesecake?"

Simply put... yes. If you have got a craving for cheesecake, then no substitute will do, it's got to be cheesecake.

### "What if I ignore my cravings?"

Realize that cravings are nothing to be afraid of. They are your body's way of telling you what it needs. Honoring this will further strengthen your intuition. If you ignore your cravings or try to fool your body by eating substitutes then your cravings will only become stronger which could lead to overeating and bingeing.

### "But, I am only craving energy dense foods!"

Please rest assured that even if you're craving a lot of cheesecake right now, it won't be long before your body tells you it wants other things like fruits, vegetables, pasta, meat and whole foods. The more you press on with intuitive eating the more you'll find you want to eat in a really balanced way.

### "This sounds scary!"

Don't worry, remember you are going to start off slowly and gradually build up your confidence with intuitive eating. To begin with all you need to do is use your intuition to guide you through one meal (or snack if you prefer) a day.

### "But what if the foods I want to eat are all really healthy anyway?"

If you find yourself intuitively wanting to eat salads, fruit or wholefoods then that is fine. Of course, if you find that this is the case all of the time then you may need to question whether you are really letting yourself be intuitive. If you're still letting those food fears hold you back then it is important to become aware of it.

Most people don't crave very healthy foods 100% of the time and it is important to allow yourself to eat any foods that you want, even if you previously considered them to be triggering or bad foods.

### "What if I don't have the food that I am craving?"

At times the food you are craving will not be accessible. In this case visualize another food that will satisfy your needs. If you are not able to visualize another food, then have something that closely resembles what you are craving. The more accurately you can satisfy your body's needs, the more satisfied you will be after your meal, thus reducing the tendency to overeat. If you find you continually crave a specific food, then it makes sense to have that food readily available.

## Summary

To begin with, for one meal a day ask yourself "what do I feel like eating?" Intuitively select foods that satisfy your cravings and give yourself permission to eat those foods, guilt free.

# Intuitive Eating Step 2:
# Eat Until You Feel Satisfied Then Stop

In this step you are going to practice stopping eating once you are comfortably full. By eating slowly and paying attention you will begin to notice the subtle sensations of satiety. Satiety indicates that you have eaten the right amount of food to fill your stomach and take away any feelings of hunger. When comfortably full you will feel light, energetic and ready for your next activity. You'll notice that as you become full, the flavor of the food goes from fabulous to just okay and it gets harder to give food and eating your full attention.

Other signs to look out for include:
- A drop in your stomach.
- A comfortable, content, warm feeling in your stomach.
- An urge that tells you that you have had enough to eat.
- A gentle, clear, satisfied sensation in the solar plexus (the area below your rib cage but above your stomach).
- A feeling of being content.
- Not feeling hungry any more.
- Not having any more food thoughts.
- You may even let out a satisfaction sigh.

Once we notice that we are satisfied we should stop eating.

**What you need to do:**
Choose one meal a day to practice listening to your satiety. Eat slowly, pay attention during the meal and keep an eye out for feelings of satisfaction. It can take up to 20 minutes for any feelings of fullness to register, so please take your time during your meal. Two thirds of the way through your meal, or as soon as you notice any feelings of satiety, pause for a moment. During this pause put your hand on your stomach and try and feel the sensations of filling up. Ask yourself "Am I truly satisfied or do I need to eat more food?" If you feel that you are truly satisfied then stop eating. Put your knife and fork down and walk away from the table.

If you are not satisfied, then imagine the feeling of being comfortably full in your stomach. This isn't overly full, this is just the right amount of food that feels good, not too heavy, not too light. Decide how much more food you think will be required to make you feel truly satisfied and then eat that amount. You may need to put more food on your plate to feel truly satisfied.

Once you have eaten that amount pause again and ask yourself "Am I truly satisfied or do I need to eat more food?" If you are truly satisfied walk away from the table, If not, continue eating until you are truly satisfied.


## FAQS

### "What if I think I've just eaten too much?"

Do not panic. This is very normal, so please do not worry. Intuitive eating is a skill and takes a lot of practice. If you feel you have eaten too much, then make sure to stop eating and walk away from the table. Do not feel guilty about eating the extra food. Understand that if you overeat at one meal, your body will naturally self-correct and you will not feel so hungry at the next meal.

### "What if I am still not full and I have finished my meal?"

If you have been paying attention and eating slowly but are still hungry, it is obvious that your body needs more food. Give yourself permission to eat more food. If the thought of eating more food makes you feel a little anxious, then feel free to wait 10 minutes. Sometimes it can take a little longer for feelings of fullness to register. If after 10 minutes you are still hungry then you know it is real hunger and you should eat.

### "What should I do with the left over food?"

If you feel that left over food may be a binge trigger then I recommend you dispose of your left over food in the trash as soon as you are finished eating. Some people feel uncomfortable with the idea of throwing food away but it is vital to safeguard your recovery in this way. Alternatively you may want to freeze the food, if it is something that you want to keep for another day.

......................................................................................................

*"I agree. Something that was powerful for me was getting rid of the leftovers from meals as soon as my family was through eating. I couldn't have the extra food staring at me and it was empowering to throw it away or down the disposal and think there*

*is another victory for today. I would say aloud to myself, "I am sorry for throwing out this good food, but it's necessary for now." - Tess*

............................................................................

### "I feel guilty for eating more food"

Do not feel guilty. As long as you are paying attention and eating slowly, then you know that it is true hunger. This is a true need. Your body needs this food. You never have to feel guilty for giving your body what it needs. Do you feel guilty for giving your body air? Do you feel guilty for giving your body water? Of course not, so don't feel guilty for giving your body the food it needs.

### "But I still feel anxious eating that amount of food"

If eating more food will cause you too much anxiety simply stop when you feel like doing so. It's much better to stop eating rather than risking purging your food.

### "What if I don't feel sensations of fullness?"

It can take time for your feelings of fullness to return. Most people reconnect with feelings of hunger a lot sooner than they reconnect with sensations of fullness, so give it time. If you don't feel any sensation of fullness, then stick to your allocated portions from your structured eating plan for now. In time the sensations will return.

### "I am hungry shortly after my meals"

Then you may need to reassess if you really were truly satisfied in the first place. Try increasing the portion size of your main meals. Also make sure you are eating a balanced meal and that you're getting enough protein. Be very careful of mind games. Do not fool yourself into thinking you are satisfied with your meal when you are not. This is another form of restrictive eating and will lead you straight back to bingeing and purging.

### "I find this too challenging!"

Spotting the signs of fullness is challenging and takes practice. There will be times when you eat too much and times when you will eat too little and this is perfectly okay. With more practice, and as you begin to understand your body better, you can confidently and accurately assess your hunger levels during a meal. The transition to intuitive eating is bumpy for everyone at first.

................................................................................................

*"Today I had a bran muffin and a small piece of chicken for lunch and was left feeling very unsatisfied. I tried chewing gum, drinking water, and going for a walk, but the urge to eat still remained. I started thinking about going out and getting a pizza to binge on. Instead, I forced myself to turn inward and ask myself what I was feeling. And honestly, the answer that came back was "hungry." So I grabbed a frozen pizza slice I had in the freezer and ate that, and I stopped there!" - Petra H*

................................................................................................

## Summary

Choose one meal a day and practice listening to your satiety. Two thirds of the way through your meal, or as soon as you notice any feelings of satiety, pause for a moment. During this pause, put your hand on your stomach and try to feel the sensations of filling up. Ask yourself "Am I truly satisfied or do I need to eat more food?" If you need more food be sure to allow yourself to eat it.

# Intuitive Eating Step 3:
# Go Fully Intuitive

Gradually we want to move towards a more fully intuitive lifestyle. To do this we need to implement the final key to becoming an intuitive eater... eat when you feel hungry.

**What you need to do:**
The final step to becoming an intuitive eater is to stop eating food every three hours and instead to eat something when you feel hungry. Rather than following the clock, trust your intuitive hunger signals. They will provide a cue as to when you should eat.

Throughout the day look out for the subtle sensations of hunger. If you feel the subtle sensations of hunger then you know that it's time to eat. If you are using the hunger scale to track your hunger you will want to eat when you are between "4. Slightly hungry" and "3. Fairly hungry."

Try to avoid playing mind games with yourself. Be careful not to fool yourself into thinking you are not hungry when you are. You need to be careful not to dismiss real hunger. This is your body's way of telling you it would like some food.

**Putting it all together.**
These are the three simple golden principles to living life as an intuitive eater.
1.   Eat when you feel hungry.
2.   Eat what you feel like eating.
3.   Stop eating when you feel comfortably satisfied.

**Going fully intuitive**
There is no right or wrong way to begin the transition to fully intuitive eating. For most people, transitioning to fully intuitive eating will require a lot of going back and forth - a lot of testing out what works best for you. Some of you will want to dive right in and go fully intuitive while others may want to stay between structured eating and intuitive eating for a few months. Both approaches are perfectly fine, just find what works best for you.

I don't want to give you any specific directions on how to go about this because you already have the answers within yourself. It's up to you to decide when and how you wish to fully embrace these principles. If it feels right for you, then it is right for you. Trust your intuition. Trust your gut. Go with what feels natural and best. Your intuition will provide you with all the insight and direction you need. As I said at the start of the book, you have everything you need within you to fully recover. It's all there. You just need to tune in and listen.

If you are looking for some ideas on how to get started with intuitive eating, you can try a few of these suggestions to see how they work for you:

- Try eating intuitively for just one day at a time whilst relying on your structured eating plan for other days. Gradually increase the number of days you eat intuitively.
- Just focus on eating until you feel satisfied but for now still choose to eat foods from your structured eating plan.
- Just focus on eating when you feel hungry but for now stick to your structured eating portion sizes.

### The final step in recovery
Going fully intuitive is the final step in your recovery from bulimia. As you practice intuitive eating you will be amazed by how much more clearly your body begins communicating with you. Your body will let you know exactly what it needs in order to experience optimal health.

Once you learn to eat intuitively you will never have to fear food again, you will never have to count calories, you will never have to restrict your food intake, fret over what you should eat or be trapped by any food rules. Food will become just food and you will be free from bulimia nervosa... forever.

## FAQs

### "Should I eat 100% intuitively?"
We are not striving for perfection here because there is no such thing, and it can be difficult for anyone to eat intuitively 100% of the time. As a guideline I would suggest eating most of your meals according to your intuition and not stressing if every now and then you find yourself eating something when you are not hungry. It's completely

normal to have times when you eat when you are not hungry; family gatherings, ice cream at the beach, popcorn at the cinema etc. This is a natural part of normal healthy eating, it is totally acceptable and should not be feared. Of course some intuitive eaters do prefer to eat 100% intuitively all of the time, and that's okay too. As your intuition gets stronger you will find that eating food when you are not hungry isn't very enjoyable. Both approaches are perfectly fine, there is no right or wrong way to do this. Listen to your intuition and find out what approach works best for you.

................................................................................................................

*"My friend actually laughed at me for turning down ice-cream on a hot day last year because I wasn't hungry, but I wasn't, so had no urge whatsoever to eat it. To me it's like sleeping when you're not tired, no "intuitive sleeper" would do that because they'd have absolutely no desire to do so."*
*- Catherine Liberty, Recovery Coach*

................................................................................................................

## "What does normal eating look like?"

Everyone is unique when it comes to eating habits but here are some indications that you are on the right path.

- Eating is often enjoyable.
- Food does not pre-occupy the majority of your thoughts.
- Eating is flexible in terms of timing and variety.
- You don't feel guilty after eating.
- You eat when you are hungry and stop when you are full.
- You have times when you eat when you are not hungry but you accept that your body will naturally self correct.
- You eat what you feel like eating.

# Intuitive Eating:
## Super Short Version

Gradually let go of your structured eating plan and instead implement these three intuitive eating rules into you life.

1.  Eat when you feel hungry.
2.  Eat what you feel like eating.
3.  Stop eating when you feel comfortably satisfied.

For guidance, tune into and trust your intuition and inner wisdom. Only you know what works best for you.

---

Don't forget you can go to **www.bulimiahelp.org/bonus** to download your Recovery Checklist which will help you to keep track of the all steps you need to follow!

---

# Lola's Success Story

" My name is Lola. I'm 34 years old and I suffered from bulimia for a year and a half before I had enough. I was bingeing and purging up to 3 or 4 times a day, abusing laxatives and an over-exerciser. It was unbelievable that I was going through this. Shouldn't I, as a 30-something know better? I would scream at myself that what I was doing was wrong and ridiculous and that I needed help! I'll stop tomorrow - this will be the last time! is what I told myself over and over.

It was following a particularly harrowing 3 or 4 days that I decided I was serious about leaving bulimia behind, like breaking up from a bad relationship or saying good-bye to an abusive friend. I didn't need or want this cycle of hell in my life.

That's when I found bulimiahelp.org. It's sad to say but in my town there were few services offered to help those with eating disorders. It was a major, positive turning point in my life...

The program saved my life! It made absolute perfect sense why I was bulimic and what had caused it. In retrospect, the restrictive eating and obsessive exercising all for the sake of losing a couple of extra kilograms was ludicrous! My body weight was stable before bulimia, but as a bulimic I went up a dress size. The answer was simple: the way to stop binge eating is to feed your body and stop purging. I found the answer I needed. It has now been ten months since the last time I purged

My relationship with food has improved ten-fold. Trigger food that I could never have in the cupboard out of fear of uncontrollable bingeing is now enjoyed in moderation!

My weight has stabilized and I am following a safe and moderate exercise regime with the guidance of an exercise physiologist. I have not put on any weight from ceasing to purge. In fact I have lost a little without even trying. My main focus and concern however is getting my health in tip-top shape!  My life and happiness is no longer ruled by a number on a scale. In fact, I threw my scales out long ago! I feel that I am in much more control of food and my destiny and some of my positivity and zest has returned. I know it will help anyone who desperately wants to start a new chapter of their life and to be happier and in control! "

– Lola

# Final Thoughts

Congratulations! You made it through.

I hope you'll now take the time to acknowledge all that you've done because it's no small task. In fact, it's really big! We've covered a lot of ground, and you stuck with me, step by step, from beginning to end.

All you have to do now is make the decision to commit to your recovery. As I said at the start of this book, you have everything you need within you right now to fully recover. You have more inner strength, power and vitality than you realize. It's all there. Trust me, you can do this. You can be free.

This may be the end of this book, but that doesn't have to mean it's the end of our work together. Your recovery is an organic, adaptive and evolving process. I look forward to continuing to serve you in the best and most effective ways I can. To that end, at BulimiaHelp.org, you can continue to receive support and advice about all of the concepts I've laid out in this book.

If you want more help, if you want to have your own Certified Bulimia Help Coach, if you want to work in a structured environment that will inspire you to take action and keep you accountable, then join one of our highly acclaimed online recovery programs.

Finally, I would now like to ask you for a favor. If you enjoyed The Bulimia Help Method, would you mind taking a minute to write a review on Amazon? Reviews have the power to make or break a book and even a short review helps. It'd mean a lot to me and it would help others to discover our program.

Also, if someone you care about is struggling with Bulimia Nervosa or disordered eating, please consider sending him or her a copy of this book. Whether you gift it to them on Amazon or email a copy of the PDF makes no difference to me.

Thank you so much for reading the Bulimia Help Method and spending time with me.

To your amazing, fantastic, wonderful recovery,

Ali Kerr & Richard Kerr
Bulimiahelp.org

# Participate in a Bulimia Help Method Support Program or 1-1 Coaching To Help Support, Guide and Motivate You Through Your Recovery.

The more support you have for your recovery the better your chances of success. At bulimiahelp.org we provide additional support via our online programs and dedicated one-to-one recovery coaching.

A BHM Recovery Coach can help:
- Support you when you fall off track or slip up.
- Troubleshoot solutions to any obstacles in recovery.
- Keep you motivated when you feel disillusioned.
- Answer your recovery questions.
- Help you meal plan.
- Guide you through the Bulimia Help Method.
- Be your rock, foundation and anchor in your recovery.
- Teach you the right mindset along with the habits and behaviors necessary for lifelong recovery.
- Guide you down the path to a full recovery.

**Learn more at http://www.bulimiahelp.org**

................................................................................

*"For 46 years until recently I've been a bulimic. That's a long time to be anything. Now I am sixty. I have seen more doctors and been in more programs than you can imagine, all to no avail. I signed up to coaching which led me out of a fiery inferno to a place where the anguish stopped and I could heal my wounds. Now I am accomplishing things I had worked so, so, so hard for my whole life. Recovery Coaching has literally saved my life, physically, mentally and in that elusive portion of our psyches, the soul. I am so grateful. If you are suffering, sign up. Every part of the program will help you, and the support is unlimited. Take it from an old timer, it is the best of the best." - Michelle*

................................................................................

# About the Authors

In 2003 Ali Kerr confessed to her husband Richard that she was suffering from bulimia nervosa. Together they sought recovery. Frustratingly, for a time, recovery remained elusive: therapy proved ineffective, doctors were not helpful and inpatient treatment unaffordable.

So with nothing left to lose, they decided to take matters into their own hands. Utilizing the research skills they'd developed at university, together they began researching, testing and questioning everything they could find on bulimia nervosa. After years of research they felt they had devised a recovery method that could really work and they later named this the 'Bulimia Help Method'. Following the method, Ali made a rapid and full recovery. Since then the Bulimia Help Method has gone on to help over 11,000 sufferers and is recommended by experts, doctors and eating disorder charities worldwide.

# Appendix 1: Recovery Timelines

I want you to be mentally prepared for recovery so I have laid out a rough timeline that will give you an idea of what to expect, and when to expect it. However, I want to emphasize that everyone's recovery is unique, so there is no need to worry if your recovery timeline is completely different.

## What to expect at the start of your recovery (Week 1)

- The first week of your recovery is likely to feel incredibly overwhelming. With so much to take in you may find yourself feeling exhausted and continually questioning your ability to recover. You may notice an increase in negative thoughts and all emotions will feel amplified.
- Some people also experience a phase of increased binge urges, but this is nothing to worry about.
- On the plus side, you will no longer feel crazy, lost or alone. You can expect to have a lot of "light bulb moments" as you begin understanding the recovery process and you'll quickly become amazed by your own strength and resilience.

## Weeks 2-3

- You will likely experience bloating as your body re-hydrates and your digestive system begins processing food properly again (bloating is especially noticeable around your stomach and parotid glands). Weight fluctuations will occur.
- Urges to binge and purge will remain and may even increase, but despite this, you'll feel so much more committed to recovery. You'll be inspired to overcome your bulimia more than ever.
- You'll most likely feel worn-out and have little energy because recovery demands so much of you. You may continue to experience rapidly changing moods, feeling on top of the world one moment, and completely depressed the next.
- You can expect to experience your first fully successful days of structured eating, and even though you switch between feeling too hungry and overly full, you'll be incredibly impressed by your ability to eat normally without turning back to bulimic behaviors.
- Despite your best efforts to implement regular eating, episodes of binging and purging may continue at this time.
- Your "bulimic-logic" may be at its worst which means you'll find that "all or nothing" ways of thinking are dominating your thought processes. At this point it's typical to still see slipping up as failing.

## Weeks 3-5

- At this time recovery feels scary, exciting and very up and down. Strong urges to binge and purge are still felt most days, especially in the evenings.
- Structured eating is still a big challenge and requires all of your attention. You can feel as though you're obsessing over food more than ever and you still have an inability to distinguish true hunger from emotional hunger.
- You're likely to have utilized some basic recovery strategies at this stage and found them helpful some of the time.
- You continue to worry about excessive weight gain and find yourself feeling paranoid that the things you're experiencing are "not normal."
- You still feel hopeless, lost, afraid and lack trust in recovery a lot of the time, but in deep contrast you occasionally feel hopeful, inspired, courageous and trust in the recovery process.

## 1-2 Months
- Initial bloating has subsided giving you a big boost of confidence and a restored faith in recovery.
- As your body begins to get all the nutrients it needs, your skin becomes more radiant, your eyes get brighter and your hair and nails become stronger.
- You're able to appreciate the benefits of structured eating, but still worry that you're eating too much food. You may find it impossible to eat certain "trigger foods" without completely losing control.
- You worry that you'll never make peace with your body but you do find it easier to avoid obsessive checking behaviors.

## 2-3 Months
- Your metabolism has increased and your weight has become more stable, but you're still prone to small fluctuations over the next couple of months.
- You've developed a brand new awareness and understand when binge urges are likely to strike.
- You're able to use several recovery strategies effectively in order to postpone or avoid bingeing all together.
- Eating is still hard work at times but has definitely become less of a battle. You're increasingly able to tell the difference between real hunger cues and emotional hunger, and you now trust the process of structured eating.
- Your relationships and social life take an upturn around this time.
- You can experience dreams about relapsing at this point in your recovery. Although scary, these dreams are actually a positive sign that you're ready to accept change on a subconscious level.

## 3-4 Months

- You're able to trust true hunger a lot more at this point, and you've finally started to experience comfortable fullness after meals. You're able to eat many different types of foods (including some previously triggering foods) without worrying about weight gain or loss of control.
- Frustratingly slow progress in developing additional coping skills coupled with negative body image makes you question your ability to recover.
- On the other hand, you're able to think with true clarity and no longer experience the trance-like states that often accompany bulimic thoughts and behaviours.
- You have a new found appreciation for the smaller things in life and your "good days" tend to completely outnumber your "bad days."

## 4-5 Months

- You feel the process of recovery is relentless and long to take a "break" from it, but at the same time you experience a brand new sense of pride based on your progress so far.
- You've finally started to grasp that recovery is a process, that it's normal to take two steps forward and one step back, and that it's okay to feel weak.
- Worries about who you truly are without bulimia begin to surface, causing additional confusion and anxiety.

## After 6 Months of recovery

- Binge urges tend to be minimal or even non-existent at this stage which offers a much needed escape from detailed planning and strategizing.
- Expect to have successfully reintroduced many or all "banned foods," and to have discovered that no food is off limits to you any more.
- You feel like celebrating your successes (and you should) and you're even inclined to talk more openly with your loved ones.
- But at this time you're also prone to complacency with your recovery, believing that you no longer need to work hard to stay on track. Letting your guard down too much can lead to relapse.
- With no binge urges expect to experience an increased desire to restrict your food in an effort to lose weight. When acting on thoughts of restriction expect almost immediate loss of control, re-emergence of bulimic urges and weight gain (yes, even a little restriction can shock your body back into a state of primal hunger).
- You still struggle with understanding your true identity. You may feel shame or guilt as you mourn the loss of your eating disorder and you'll feel great disappointment that you haven't fully recovered.
- Expect to have days where you feel like you've fully recovered, only to experience bumps in the road the following day.

## 7-8 Months

- You're now completely confident in your ability to overcome relapses and you know that bulimia no longer numbs your feelings or offers the emotional escape that it once did.
- You've reached your set point weight and you're comfortable around food most of the time.
- You still rely on forward planning and strategies to make it through more challenging days and situations.
- You are a lot more intuitive with your food choices.
- You no longer feel the urge to rush through recovery and you'll likely find yourself fully accepting of the time it takes to recover.
- Your moods are stable, you feel alive and you notice a new sense of self-confidence and body acceptance developing.

## 9 Months

- At this stage recovery doesn't seem so bad after all. You've learned the value of gradual change and you've managed to truly let go of your fear of relapse.
- You still experience thoughts about restriction and dieting from time to time, but you are confident in your ability to let such thoughts wash over you without acting on them.
- You need to remain mindful of eating regularly, but it's no longer the effort that it once was.
- You feel a new sense of peace. Long forgotten interests start making themselves known and discovering your true personality is no longer scary, it's exciting!
- You experience true self-confidence and urges to nurture yourself.
- Relapses are rare at this stage, but if they do happen you're able to get back on track with recovery almost immediately.

## 12 Months of recovery (and beyond)

- You'll feel like you're almost there at this point.
- You'll rely on recovery strategies sparingly, as new healthy habits, behaviors and coping strategies have become natural and instinctive.
- From time to time you still experience fleeting negative thoughts, but they have no control over your actions and no longer cause anxiety.
- Confidence in your ability to master intuitive eating continues to grow over the following months and you finally make the switch from structured eating.
- You experience a strong sense of peace, contentment and wholeness and you're often overwhelmed with positivity when focusing on the reality of how far you have come.
- Expect to want to share your recovery with everyone, because it seems like it was only yesterday when you felt hopeless, lost and alone.

# A Real Life Recovery Time Line

Here is a  real life recovery timeline from one of our previous members, Claire.

### Claire's Recovery Timeline:

"I consider May 20th, 2011 my "quit date" even though I binged and purged several times after that line in the sand. It was on May 20th that I made the decision to always be in recovery for bulimia, regardless of my behaviors. From that moment on, I actively worked towards quitting and made the commitment to never again put off recovery, not even for 2 hours. It took 6 months until the bingeing subsided and my weight was back to normal (it went up in the first months of recovery). By the 9th month, I had actually lost weight!

This is my timeline:

### Month 1:

Everything was about not bingeing or purging. It was really hard. I felt like I was overeating. I isolated myself a lot, but I made sure to take care of myself. I didn't weigh myself. No bingeing or purging.

### Month 2:

Weight gain was really upsetting, but I felt proud to see my behaviors becoming more normal. A few episodes of bingeing and purging.

### Months 3 and 4:

I started running, and that made me feel a lot better. My weight was still higher than normal and I didn't feel attractive. I didn't make efforts to date or hang out. It was a lonely time, but I felt very proud of myself. My self-respect was growing and I was much more peaceful because my finances were straightening out. I slept a lot. Occasional bingeing and purging.

### Months 5 and 6:

My mood improved and I dropped a little weight, bringing me back to the weight I was when I'd been bingeing and purging. My energy increased. I felt alive and optimistic again. Very few cases of bingeing and purging.

### Months 7 and 8:

In month 7, I experienced my last binge/ purge!! These were my miracle months!!!! I revel in the memories. :) All my cravings went away and I began eating like a "normal" person. I was able to keep food in the house. I no longer struggled with the urge to binge. I felt happy and light. It was like I was reconnecting with some woman who'd started to develop years and years ago but whose life got cut off due to bulimia.

### Months 9 and 10:

It was very surprising to me and of some concern to my therapist, but I lost more weight! I was (and still am) astonished. It's true then. Bulimia had been keeping me at a weight that was HIGHER than my set-point! During these months I did a lot of planning and dreaming and preparing for the next stages of my life. I re-evaluated my job, relationships, apartment decor, hairstyle, habits, everything... I was getting very excited about my future.

### Months 11 and 12:

Still maintaining the lower weight without any food cravings, even during PMS. I'm in the process of getting a new job - even considering a career change - and I've started dating again. For the first time in my life, I'm dating really upstanding men, men of true character. I know it's because I respect myself and I've gotten a grip on what really matters. I'm very, very grateful. I still have emotional lows, but my worst days now are better than my best days as a bulimic.

The thing I want to emphasize is that a year is a really long period of time and a lot can change in a year. It might feel like your recovery isn't happening quickly enough, but take a step back and keep the big picture in mind. When I was frustrated by my "slow" (in my mind) progress, I would always, always ask myself, "10 years down the road, will it matter if I took 3 months or 13 months to get better?" Of course not! I'd had bulimia for 11 years and I was willing to be patient. If I hadn't been patient and instead fell prey to 'all or nothing' thinking, I might still be bulimic. I might have been bulimic for another 10 years! What a horrible thought! Recovery is possible! It can happen!" - Claire

"You can recover. I believe in you."

30292059R00117

Made in the USA
Middletown, DE
19 March 2016